CHURCHILL
a founder of modern
IRELAND

ANTHONY J. JORDAN

I would like to thank staffs of the following libraries who assisted in the work: Royal Dublin Society, National Library, Pembroke, Ringsend. I also received help from Vera Brown, Pat O'Keefe, Judith Jordan and Fiona Jordan.

Copyright Anthony J Jordan 1995

ISBN 0 9524447 0 4

This book is dedicated to:

Lance Corporal Thomas Kedian, 10th Battalion Lancashire Fusiliers (step-brother and godfather to my mother Delia Jordan), who died, at the Somme, aged twenty six, on 7 July 1916, and whose grave is unknown, but is commemorated on the Thiepval Memorial in France.

AND

The pupils of Sandymount School-Clinic, with whom parts of this story were enjoyed.

We wish to thank the following for permission to use material:

Public Record Office Richmond Surrey for Cover Photograph, "Prime Minister's Call". Inf 2/73 p.37.

Oxford University Press for "Whitehall Diary" by Thomas Jones.

Office of Public Works Dublin for Gough Monument Photograph.

Dublin Civic Museum for Photograph of Theatre Royal Fire.

While every effort has been made to contact copyright holders we have failed to contact some. Westport Books will be happy to come to some arrangement with these should they wish to contact us.

I would like to thank the British Ambassador, Mr. Christopher Blatherwick for reading the manuscript.

Published by Westport Books

CONTENTS

Chapter	Title	Page
	INTRODUCTION	5
1	CHILDHOOD IN DUBLIN	7
2	AT WARS WITH THE IRISH	15
3	A POLITICIAN TO WATCH	23
4	LET ULSTER FIGHT FOR THE DIGNITY AND HONOUR OF IRELAND	32
5	APPEASING THE UNIONISTS	47
6	AN UNHAPPY WAR FOR WINSTON	58
7	GET THREE GENERALS IF YOU CANNOT GET THREE JUDGES	66
8	YOU SAW DEVALERA WITHOUT ANY PRECONDITIONS	78
9	NEGOTIATING WITH THE REBELS	91
10	DEALING WITH COLLINS AND CRAIG	106
11	SECURING THE PEACE	118
12	FOUNDER OF THE IRISH FREE STATE	136
13	THE ILLUSORY BOUNDARY COMMISSION	151
14	CHURCHILL'S FEARS CONFIRMED	160
15	SECOND WORLD WAR	169
16	TWO ELDER STATESMEN	188
	SOURCES	201
	INDEX	206

Winston, aged five, in Ireland

INTRODUCTION

Winston Churchill was an old fashioned English patriot of the imperial era. Though the interests of the home country determined his attitude in political and military affairs, he was never slow to be critical should the need arise, even switching political parties on occasion. His lonely childhood led to a bumptious and aggressive personality which was happiest in frenzied activity, preferably of a military nature. He married sensibly and led a stable family life producing five children. He was a democrat who had a history of being rejected by the electorate, but always returned to claim his seat in Parliament.

Despite his heavy worldwide political commitments, he had a long connection with Ireland, firstly through his Grandfather and Father. His earliest memories were of Ireland and his most formative years were spent there, in an anti- Catholic and anti-Irish environment. As a politician he was firmly against Home Rule for Ireland at first, regarding that country as an integral part of the Kingdom. But for political reasons he adopted the Home Rule policy and fought for its passage in Parliament, before the First World War. As, Secretary of State for the Army and Navy, he felt that the rebellion in Ireland during the Anglo-Irish War had to be suppressed at all costs, as Parliament had already ruled on the matter in the Government of Ireland Act 1920. When the Truce came he played a major part in the Treaty negotiations. As Secretary of State for the Colonies, he was then instrumental in buttressing the new Irish Free State, cajoling, convincing, intimidating the Irish leaders towards implementing the Treaty. One biographer has called him the Founder of Ireland. When the fiasco of the Boundary Commission had to be sorted out, it was Churchill, as Chancellor of the Exchequer, who got that task.

DeValera and the republicans were anathema to Churchill. They proved his foreboding correct, particularly by the policy of neutrality during Britain's darkest days of the Second World War, when the ports so foolishly handed over in appeasement by Joseph Chamberlain, according to Churchill's view, were denied to Britain.

But the Unionists of Northern Ireland proved their faithful friendship. In his moment of greatest victory on V.E. day, Churchill unwisely attacked DeValera affording him the opportunity to make a devastating reply. The Declaration of a Republic and the complete break with the Commonwealth were for Churchill, symptoms of a wider malaise in the breakup of the old British Empire. But at least Northern Ireland remained faithful and was rewarded appropriately, in the Ireland Act 1949, putting a united Ireland, outside the Commonwealth, almost out of sight.

In the early nineteen fifties both Churchill and DeValera found themselves in office after periods in Opposition. On Churchill's invitation, the two old and ailing men, met for lunch at ten Downing Street. Churchill said afterwards, "I like the man".

CHAPTER 1

CHILDHOOD IN DUBLIN

Winston Churchill's earliest memories were of Ireland. He was taken to live there while a little boy and spent three formative years living in Dublin's Phoenix Park. His house was called 'The Little Lodge'. It was surrounded by bushes, which to his eyes looked like woods, even a forest. While there he learned that the Irish, called Fenians, were a dangerous and ungrateful lot, who murdered his friends and refused to say thanks for assistance rendered them. The Churchill family had gone to Ireland unwillingly and were rather pleased to escape from the place, where it always seemed to be raining. The cause of the family exile lay in a confrontation, Winston's father had with Royalty.

The Little Lodge, Phoneix Park, where Winston lived as a boy. It is now the National Civil Defence H.Q. and backs onto Aras an Uachtarain.

Queen Victoria's son, the Prince of Wales, was a notorious rake. On occasions he absented himself from Britain and caroused abroad with a select group of friends. In 1875 the Prince left for India. Among his party was Lord Aylesford, another rake. While the latter was away his wife ran off with Blandford Churchill, a brother of Randolph Churchill, father of Winston. Lord Aylesford threatened to divorce his wife. This would have ruined her and Blandford Churchill. Randolph intervened to protect his brother. He threatened to reveal incriminating letters in his possession which had passed between the Prince of Wales and Lady Aylesford. Queen Victoria called in her Prime Minister, Disraeli, as she feared a political scandal. The outcome for the Churchill family was that they were to be boycotted by the Monarchy. Disraeli advised Randolph's father, the Duke of Marlborough, to leave the country and to take Randolph with him. There was a vacancy as Lord Lieutenant - Viceroy - in Ireland which Disraeli offered to the Duke. It was with great reluctance that the Duke accepted this post. The salary was £20,000, but it cost a minimum of £40,000 each year to fulfill the duties involved. The Duke had to sell some of the treasures of Blenheim Palace and shut the place up for the duration of his Irish exile. Queen Victoria graciously agreed to receive the Duke and Duchess before their departure, on the proviso that the unpleasant business with their two sons would not be mentioned.

On the 12th December 1876 the Duke, accompanied by his son Randolph, arrived at Kingstown from Holyhead where a special train took the party as far as Westland Row. A carriage then took them to the Chief Secretary's Lodge, from where they later drove to Dublin Castle. There amid great pomp, the Duke was received by the Lords Justice and Privy Council and inducted into his office, receiving salutes of fifteen guns and twenty one guns, fired from the ordinance in the Phoenix Park. The Duke and Randolph later returned to England to make final preparations for the entire family to make the transfer to Ireland.

Shortly afterwards the Churchills left London in a special saloon carriage attached to the Irish Limited Mail. They departed Holyhead that same evening aboard the steamer Connaught, arriving at Kingstown shortly after ten o'clock, and anchored for the night in the Man-of-War Roads. The next day the new Viceroy, in full uniform, made a glittering State Entry into Dublin with a large entourage. The London Times reported that the party "received a loyal and hearty welcome from the citizens of all classes and denominations". The Times incorrectly described Winston as Lord Winston Spencer Churchill and his three accompanying Aunts, as his sisters. Master Winston, sat between his mother, Jennie Jerome and father in their own carriage. Lord Randolph, though still an M.P., was to act as his father's unpaid secretary. The Duke lived in the Vice-Regal Lodge, in the Phoenix Park, while Randolph and his family lived nearby in a large house, called the Little Lodge.

The first clear memory Winston retained, was of his grandfather unveiling a statue to Lord Gough in 1878 on the main road running through the Park. He recalled the scene vividly as the Viceroy addressed the crowd using the phrase, 'and with a withering volley he shattered the enemy's line'.

Another event Winston remembered clearly, gives us an early glimpse into his character. One Christmas he was being taken to the pantomime at the Theatre Royal. They drove the three miles into Dublin Castle at the city centre, where they were to meet with others. He remembered clearly the Castle yard as the busy place it then was. But horror of horrors, a message arrived that there was a huge fire at the theatre and

THE GOUGH STATUE: unveiled in 1880 in the Phoneix Park by Winston's Grandfather. This event provided the earliest memory for the four year old boy. The monument was destroyed in an explosion in 1957.

they were unable to proceed. Winston was told that the fire was so fierce that the building was burned to the ground and the manager with it. He was told that the only remains of the manager were the keys of the theatre which had been in his pocket. He was promised as a special treat, he would be taken to see the burnt out building the next day. But his only interest was to see the keys which had survived. This historical event was commemorated in a contemporary painting, which can be seen in Dublin's Civic Museum. The pantomime being performed was 'Ali Baba and the Forty Thieves'.

Though Winston was still an only child in the Little Lodge, he seems to have had only occasional contact with either of his parents. He saw them as they left or returned from hunts. Sometimes he could recall great scares occurring as either of them would be hours late returning from a hunt. His mother looked beautiful in her riding gear and he loved her, but from a distance. He once threathened to run after the train and jump in, if his mother should leave again. Jennie loved Ireland and found the people she mixed among genial and witty. She sometimes referred in her letters, to Winston as being obstreperous. Mentioning that she had finally acceded to her son's demand for a toy elephant, she wrote that he pronounced the word 'ephelant'. Early in 1877 the boy's first efforts at writing a 'W' begin to appear on Jennie's letters.

The person who raised Winston during these and subsequent years was called Mrs Everest, though she was unmarried. One letter Jennie wrote to her absent husband spoke of Mrs Everest, 'bothering me' about Winston's shabby clothes. Another tells how Winston protested about his mother leaving him. Mrs Everest was his confidante, his nurse, his mother in all but

Firemen from the South William Street station attending a fire that destroyed the Theatre Royal in Hawkins Street, Dublin in 1880. This watercolour in the Dublin Civic Museum confirms Winston's recollection of the event.

name. She was always with him as he played or went for trips in the Phoenix Park. She warned him about the dangerous Fenians, who might kill him, if the opportunity arose. Once when he was riding a donkey in the park they saw a group of marching men in the distance. Mrs Everest thought they might be Fenians and said so to the little boy. The donkey took fright and started kicking. Winston was thrown off and concussed. Mrs Everest was no friend of Catholics either. She believed that if the truth were known, the Pope was behind the Fenians.

Winston recalled one trip he made to the country. Lord Portarlington, who was a distant relation, had his seat at Emo Park in Kings County. They visited there once and years later, Churchill was able to remember the place clearly. He recalled a 'tall white stone tower' at the end of a long drive, which had been blown up by Cromwell. The fact that Cromwell had a reputation for blowing up things enhanced his name for the boy, as a very great man. The extended family also spent winters in the country, renting out Lord Sligo's Westport House and Knockdrin Castle in Meath.

The most difficult days of Winston's Irish sojourn were to do with his education. A Governess was employed to teach him reading, writing and sums. At first he tried hiding in the woods when she arrived, but everybody conspired against him and he was forced to attend class. The bane of his life became sums, as the Governess insisted that they could only be right or wrong, nearly right was no good. Even his mother involved herself in sums. The name of his first reading book was - Reading Without Tears.

The Chief Secretary also lived in the Phoenix Park. His Under-Secretary was a man named T.H. Burke. He would often come upon Mrs. Everest and the boy on their walks in the park. On one occasion Mr. Burke gave Winston the present of a drum.

This was an exciting toy for any child and Winston beat it all round the Little Lodge. Two years later, Winston was told that a new Chief Secretary, Mr. Cavendish, and Mr. Burke were walking in the park when they were set upon by a group of Fenians and stabbed to death. Winston thought how lucky it was that the Fenians never caught him while he was in the park.

While acting as his father's secretary in Dublin, Randolph Churchill continued to attend the House of Commons in London. He and Jennie saw clearly the shocking lot of the Irish peasantry.

Mrs. Everest

They both became friends of Isaac Butt, the leader of the Irish Home Rule Party. This was embarrassing for the Viceroy, especially when Randolph made a speech in England saying that the Tory Party should grapple with the Irish problem.

In a subsequent interview with the Morning Post Randolph made it clear that he believed Ireland was misgoverned since the Act of Union in 1800. This did not endear him to his own party or his leader Disraeli.

Jennie made many friends among the riding fraternity. She became pregnant and gave birth to another boy - John Strange Churchill - on 4 February 1880. One of her most ardent admirers and a friend of the Dukes', was named John Strange Jocelyn. The boy's paternity gave cause for much gossip as he did not have any of the characteristics of his brother or

Randolph. A sister of Jennie's, Leonie Jerome, came from America to stay at the Vice Regal Lodge. While there she met the son of Sir John Leslie of Castle Leslie, Glaslough, County Monaghan. Five years later they married, establishing a family tie between Churchill and Ireland.

Winston later recalled that his Grandfather, the Duke, had to spend all his own money on entertaining in Ireland and resented this. His Grandmother too was involved socially in Ireland and organised a fundraising campaign called, 'The Famine Fund' which raised the enormous sum of £117,000. His father spent one winter on a tour of the entire country assisting with the distribution of food, clothing and seed. But Winston said that the Irish never acknowledged any of these efforts. "It was borne upon me" he wrote, "that the Irish were a very ungrateful people".

At the General Election in 1880, the Liberal Party under William Gladstone came to power. Randolph Churchill held his parliamentary seat by sixty votes. But the Liberal victory meant that the Duke of Marlborough's tenure in Dublin was summarily ended. Randolph and his family, still to be ostracised by royalty for several years, moved back to London.

CHAPTER 2

AT WARS WITH THE IRISH

At the age of seven Winston was sent to a preparatory school near Ascot, where he received regular beatings from the school Headmaster and fellow pupils. Afterwards he went to Harrow School, where he impressed as a stubborn boy, interested mainly in the cadet corps and fencing. Here he also received beatings from the Headmaster for poor behaviour. One of his contemporaries, Desmond Morton, described him as a 'howling cad'. Though only five and a half feet tall, Winston was a pugnacious young man. At the age of eighteen he entered Sandhurst Military Academy. He graduated from there just before his father's death and joined the 4th Hussars. This was a fine cavalry regiment, entry to which had been secured through the good offices of Colonel Brabazon, an Irish landlord, who himself had gained promotion through cultivating royalty. A fellow officer accused Winston of homosexual practice in the Hussars. In a letter to his mother he spoke of how potentially fatal for his future career, the episode could have been. Winston sued for defamation and settled out of court for £500. His father had wanted him to remain in the army and out of politics, which he felt had treated himself so poorly. But Winston was now a free agent intent on vindicating his father's career.

Randolph had been dying slowly from advanced syphilis, unknown to Winston. Earlier at the height of Randolph's political career, after instigating the downfall of Gladstone's

Government in 1886, he was appointed as Chancellor of the Exchequer in Lord Salisbury's Conservative Government. But he was a reckless man and resigned impetuously, hoping that the party would rally to him and make him Prime Minister. This did not occur and he never held high office again. He was bitter, feeling betrayed by the party he had helped to power.

Shortly after his father's death, news came that Mrs Everest, who had been let go in poor circumstances by the Churchills, and who then lived in Scotland, was dying. Winston rushed to her bedside and remained with her until she lost consciousness. He told his mother that he would never know such a friend again. He and his brother, Jack, paid for the headstone. Winston arranged that fresh flowers were placed on the grave on every anniversary of her death.

MILITARY ADVENTURES

Winston craved some military action, but everywhere there was peace. A war of liberation began in Cuba and Winston had five months winters leave due. With a friend he went to New York City, where an Irishman named Bourke Cockran, a local Congressman, and one of Jennie Churchill's many lovers, met the two adventurers. Cockran put them up and entertained them lavishly. Winston was very impressed by Cockran's staccato style of speech delivery and he began to model his own delivery on Cockran's.

After a week in New York the pair made their way to Cuba, where they were welcomed as guests of the Spanish army. There Winston saw his first military action and was happy to be a participant. He won a decoration for gallantry. The American and British press criticised him for becoming involved in a war he knew nothing about. As was to be so often the case, Winston had a second string to his bow, as he was also reporting on the war for the Daily Graphic. His articles seemed to be favourable to the insurgents and embarrassed his Spanish hosts.

Winston's main aim was to get into politics. Aged twenty one, he wrote to his mother that he felt a uniting of Lord Rosebury (Liberal Prime Minister after Gladstone) and the Tory Joseph Chamberlain, would serve the country well politically. It would make a new centre party cutting out the "Fenians" and elements of the Tories. "I am a Liberal in all but name" he wrote, "were it not for Irish Home Rule - to which I will never consent - I would enter Parliament as a Liberal. As it is - Tory democracy will have to be the standard under which I will range myself".

It was while at the Goodwood Races that Winston heard that the Pathan tribesmen on the North west border of India and Afghanistan had revolted. A Field Force of three brigades were formed under an old Irish friend of his, Sir Bindon Blood, who had promised to take him on his next campaign. Winston got the job of Press Officer in the Malakand Field Force Campaign. He also acted as a correspondent for the Daily Telegraph. This did not preclude him from participating fully in the action where he showed recklessness in pursuit of gallantry awards, which he hoped would boost his ambitions to become a politician. Blood wrote of him, "He saw more fighting than I expected. He was personally engaged in some very serious work...using a rifle which he borrowed from a seriously wounded man".

His next project was to seek to join General Kitchener in Egypt and the Sudan. Kitchener was another Irishman, from County Kerry, but one who disliked the way Churchill was able to use his upper class contacts to join various campaigns. Though Winston's mother, Jennie, who knew Kitchener personally, wrote on her son's behalf, Kitchener replied that he was inundated with such requests and simply had no room to accept her son. The Prime Minister, Lord Salisbury read Winston's account of the Malakand Campaign and had a lengthy meeting with the young man. Desperate to go to the Sudan, Churchill got the Prime Minister to intercede with Kitchener. But Kitchener still refused, realising well that Churchill was merely using the army for his journalistic and political careers. Finally Winston contacted a Lady Jeune who was a friend of the Adjutant-General, Sir Evelyn Wood. This lady considered that Kitchener needed to be put in his place and used her influence to so effect. Within two days Winston was invited to join the 21st Lancers for the Sudan Campaign. Though Winston participated in the famous cavalry charge at the battle of Omduran, which saw ten thousand Dervishes killed, he was not surprised there was no mention of him in dispatches. Kitchener became a national hero. But later Winston wrote a book - The River War - which criticised Kitchener for not sparing any prisoners and for desecrating the tomb of the Mahdi (A holy man in Islamic Tradition who had led the revolt against the British). In Cairo, en route for England, Churchill visited a wounded friend of his who needed a skin graft. The Irish doctor suggested he take the skin off Winston, who immediately agreed. The doctor cut a piece of skin off his arm with a razor. His newspaper articles had made Winston very well known. During his frequent trips home he began to court the Conservative Party. His journalism was often critical of the army and this was resented in the army. The Prince of Wales, Queen Victoria's son, advised him against military journalism. In May 1899 Winston decided to resign his commission. In July he was selected as a Conservative candidate for a by election in Oldham in Lancashire, but he lost the contest.

THE BOER WAR

In October the Boer War broke out when the Boers invaded Natal. Winston, with a lucrative contract from the Morning Post and a letter of introduction from the Colonial Secretary, Joseph Chamberlain, set out for Capetown. His luggage contained a trunk full of the finest drink. Arriving at Capetown the news was bad. Within one month the irregular Boer Army, assisted by two Volunteer Irish Brigades, had beaten the mighty British army. As usual Winston was keen to get to the scene of battle. He sailed again for Durban and set out for Ladysmith which was under siege by the Boers. He got as close as thirty miles from the city but then had to billet with a party of Dublin Fusiliers at the village of Estcourt. The Boers were in control of much of the territory having defeated the British at Dundee in late October. Winston was soon writing home: "It is astonishing how we have underestimated these people. Were they less ambitious they would be more formidable. If they said 'let us crush Ladysmith - a month would do it'. This echoes accounts of the siege of Ladysmith written by Major John MacBride, a co-Leader of one of the Irish Brigades. He wrote : "The English were beaten and panicked, their cavalry trampling over the fleeing infantry and wounded and killed".

John MacBride was an Irish separatist who along with Arthur Griffith set up an Irish Society in Johannesburg as a focal point for Irish ex-patriots to meet. Griffith was a journalist who admired Boer culture. He returned to Dublin where he founded Sinn Fein, which was to supplant British rule in Ireland in 1918. He found himself arguing across the table at Ten Downing St. with Churchill at the Anglo-Irish Treaty negotiations on the similarities of the South African situation and the Irish push for freedom. The leader of another Irish

Brigade was Arthur Lynch. He was involved because he believed passionately that the cause of the Boers was a just one. The Irish Brigades were multi national forces. To complicate matters there was also an Irish Brigade fighting as an integral part of the British army. Indeed this had strange repercussions as MacBride wrote after the battle at Dundee:

"Colonel Moller and forty of his Dublin Fusiliers and Irish Fusiliers were driven into a cattle pen and forced to surrender. A number of the Irish Brigade had been at school with some of the captured men, a humiliating position all round".

Churchill was anxious to see some action though he was told it was most dangerous to move about at Estcourt. It was decided that two companies of Dublin Fusiliers would go on a reconnoitring mission aboard a train. Winston was invited to accompany them. The train was ambushed and derailed. Many were killed and the rest captured. Winston tried to escape and was nearly shot. He then tried to gain his freedom by claiming he was a journalist. But evidence was given that he took part in the action and he was sent to Praetoria with the others as a prisoner. He spent his twenty eighth birthday there. He proceeded to send letters to all and sundry seeking his freedom as a non combatant, including Bourke Cockran in New York. His capture was splashed all over the papers. Eventually General Joubert, the Boer officer, agreed to his release. But before Winston could be released he escaped. He had been in custody about a month. He eventually made a triumphant return to Durban. His capture and escape made him famous. He immediately returned to the scene of his capture at Chieveley to ask General Buller for an army commission while still reporting the war. He also asked and got a commission for his brother. Buller was preparing to attack the Boers at Colenso and along the river Tugela with a view to relieving Ladysmith.

Churchill's request was granted. He witnessed the destruction of a massive British army as the irregular Boers, including the Irish Brigade, slaughtered their enemy. Churchill wrote of the battle along the Tugela:

"The infantry, General Hart's Irish Brigade leading, filed and wound along the railway line, losing a lot of men at exposed points..it was four o'clock when the Irish Brigade began to toil up the steep sides of what is now called Inniskilling Hill, the assault was delivered by the Inniskillings and Dublin Fusiliers. The spectacle was tragic... Up the bare grassy slopes climbed the brown figures and glinting bayonets of the Irishmen, and the rattle of intense musketry drummed in our ears. The climbing figures dwindled; they ceased to move; they vanished into the hillside. Out of twelve hundred men who assaulted, both colonels, three majors, twenty officers and six hundred soldiers had fallen or were wounded. The repulse was complete". These debacles had a huge effect on Churchill who was in the position to tell the public in England what was really happening. He told The Morning Star:

"We must face the facts. The individual Boer mounted in suitable country is worth from three to five regular soldiers. The power of modern rifles is so tremendous that frontal attacks must often be repulsed. The extraordinary mobility of the enemy protects his flanks. The only way of treating the problem is either to get men equal in character and intelligence to the riflemen or, failing that, huge masses of troops".

The latter strategy is what the army did with Lord Roberts and Lord Kitchener taking over from General Buller. Winston sought new accreditation. Kitchener, not unnaturally objected to him. But as usual, Winston's contacts overcame all obstacles. The war then became a dirty war with the British adopting a scorched earth policy. The Boers had to adopt a guerilla-war strategy where local knowledge was paramount. In these circumstances the Irish Brigade was stood down and the volunteers given passage to America and Europe. John MacBride went to Paris and later to Dublin - his service for the Boers would later be a telling factor in his execution by the British army after the Dublin Easter Rising in 1916. Churchill defended the new policy of the Army as it put thousands of Boer women and children into concentration camps where very many died. He wrote to the Times on 25 June 1901 saying that he was, "honestly believing that upon the whole they involve the minimum of suffering to the unfortunate people for whom we have made ourselves responsible". But Churchill too, soon left South Africa believing that the war was about to end.

Arthur Lynch, the leader of another Irish Brigade, had been elected an M.P. for the Irish Parliamentary Party from a Galway constituency in 1901, while still in South Africa with the Boers. When he returned from there in June 1902, he was arrested and charged with high treason. Churchill was instrumental in having the House of Commons move against Lynch, and have him disfranchised until the end of the parliamentary session. Lynch was convicted and spent a year in jail. When Lynch was released in February 1904 to continue as an M.P., Churchill wrote to him : 'It was repellent to me that after the conclusion of the war, you should be imprisoned as a felon for acts which however reprehensible, involve in my opinion, at any rate, no moral turpitude: and I therefore am glad to be able to congratulate you upon regaining your liberty'. Writing of the Boers later Churchill said: "They were the most good-hearted enemy I have ever fought against in the four continents in which it has been my fortune to see service".

CHAPTER 3

A POLITICIAN TO WATCH

The Liberal Party was split on the continuing Boer War. The Conservative Government thought it opportune to call a General Election. The election was turned into a referendum on the war. It was called the 'Khaki Election' fought on the theme of backing the brave soldiers in the field. Winston was selected as a Conservative candidate for Oldham, near Manchester. He received an ecstatic welcome on his arrival in the town. As usual, he was able to call on influential people to help him. Joseph Chamberlain, the Secretary of State for the Colonies, came to Oldham to speak on his behalf. In the event Winston was elected, though only by a margin of two hundred and thirty votes. His personal popularity just pulled him through.

Churchill was not a wealthy man. He was often in debt. He now saw an opportunity to make some badly needed money. He went on a major lecture tour on the Boer War, entitled, "The War as I saw it". Dublin was included on his itinerary. While there, he revisited the Little Lodge and was "astonished to find that the lawn was only about sixty yards across, that the forests were little more than bushes, and that it only took a minute to ride to it from the Viceregal Lodge", where he was staying. He then took his lecture tour to America and Canada, emphasising to Bourke Cockran in New York, that this visit was purely for commercial reasons. There was much pro-Boer support in the U.S.A., so that Winston had to be circumspect. He did manage to meet President McKinley, Vice President-elect Theodore Roosevelt and the writer Mark Twain, on his journey. On his return to England, his total income from the tour was £5,382. This was also about the amount of his journalistic income. He had been very successful.

Queen Victoria had died while Winston was abroad and it was King Edward who opened the new Parliament in February 1901. The King spoke about the Boer War, where peace was proving elusive. Kitchener now had supreme command and the war of attrition got more vile.

The first division in the Commons occurred on the day of opening with the Prime Minister, Arthur Balfour, proposing that peers should not be allowed to take part in parliamentary elections. The Liberals and the Irish Party voted against the measure. They were joined by Churchill, who voted against his own Party. This was the first parliamentary manifestation that he could never be relied upon to follow a party line on anything. He would always vote the way he himself felt was correct. He was, and remained fundamentally, a national politician, rather than a party political one.

Four days later Winston decided he would make his maiden speech, on the Boer War. He prepared many drafts and finally learned his speech by heart. David Lloyd George, a Welsh Liberal M.P., who was violently anti-war spoke before him, causing Chamberlain to walk out. Winston took the same seat occupied by his father, when he had made his bitter resignation speech in earlier days. His mother and four aunts were in the Ladies Gallery. Winston backed his party's conduct of the war saying that it, "has been on the whole carried out with unusual humanity and generosity". He also commented: "If I were a Boer, I hope I should be fighting in the field". This drew cheers from the Irish Party who were pro-Boer.

Winston later added, "It is wonderful that the honourable members who form the Irish Party, should find it in their hearts to speak and act as they do, in regard to a war in which so much has been accomplished by the courage, the sacrifice, and, above all by, the military capacity of Irishmen. A practical reason, which I trust the honourable members will not think it presumptious in me to bring to their notice, is that they would be well advised cordially to cooperate with His Majesty's Government in bringing the war to a speedy conclusion, because they must know that no Irish question or agitation can possibly take hold on the imagination of the people of Great Britain, so long as all our thoughts are with the soldiers who are fighting in South Africa".

His speech was well received in all quarters. Joseph Chamberlain said: "Friends and intimates of his father will have welcomed the speech with utter satisfaction in the hope that we may see the father repeated in the son". It was accepted that he would be a major player in politics. Winston himself wrote of the event: "I was up before I knew it... I got through it. The Irish - whom I had been taught to detest - were a wonderful audience. They gave just the opposition which would help and said nothing they thought would disturb. They did not seem the least offended when I made a joke at their expense".

THE HOOLIGANS

Very quickly Winston proved himself to be his father's son. He became critical of his own party, even forming a ginger group with some of his high born Tory friends. They were dubbed The Hooligans. They liked to do business at dinner parties, inviting leading politicians from the Liberal Party, like Lord Rosebury and Herbert Asquith to dine with them. Winston became critical of the Government's conduct of the Boer War, especially when it dismissed General Buller, who had been so good to him and his brother. In April 1902, Winston and his Hooligans, voted against the Government when Kitchener tried, under martial law in South Africa, to stop a man he had charged with libelling him, from travelling to England. In July Arthur Balfour became Prime Minister, but did not offer Churchill any government post. The following year Joseph Chamberlain split the Tory Party by declaring for Tariffs and against Free Trade, which had been the party gospel. Churchill told Balfour that the Party's position was making him reconsider his position in politics. He became a firm advocate of Free Trade and supported a Liberal Party Free Trade candidate against his own Party in a by election, saying, "Thank God, we have a Liberal Party". This led to his own Unionist - Tory constituency in Oldham voting no confidence in him. He then began to court the Liberal Party for a constituency. In March he and a fellow Hooligan, Jack Seely, resigned from the Conservative Party.

CROSSES FLOOR OF COMMONS

The following month Winston was asked to stand for the Liberals in Manchester, a centre of Free Trade. Writing to the President of the North West Manchester Liberal Association, he said "... I remain of the opinion that the creation of a separate Parliament for Ireland, would be dangerous and impracticable". D.A.Thomas Liberal M.P. for Merthyr Burghs, who had earlier offered Winston support in his quest for a nomination in Cardiff, wrote to Winston saying he had offered his support," in the belief that you had abandoned the errors of your party, and were fully prepared to come over to our side. I fear...my disappointment in observing the attitude you continue to adopt towards such cardinal principles of Liberal policy as those relating to Irish Home Rule, Disestablishment of the English Church and the House of Lords".

On 31 May Churchill took the momentous decision to cross the floor of the Commons and sit with the Liberals. He sat in the same seat occupied by his father while in opposition, beside the man he would work with for many years, Lloyd George. This move of Winston's was again laying the ghost of his father, who, though betrayed by the Unionist-Tories, had not been able to leave them. It was a move filled with risk, as it made him a continuing figure of hate for his erstwhile Party. But he proved a dogged debater and began to flay the Government with criticism. At one stage the P.M., Balfour retorted: "It is not desirable to come into this House with invective, which is both prepared and violent". This speech occurred after the Government was defeated on an amendment to the Irish Land Act. Balfour said he would not resign or dissolve Parliament. This led to the violent attack on him by Churchill. Later Chamberlain criticised his own P.M. and Balfour resigned. The King invited the sixty nine year old Henry Campbell-Bannerman, Liberal Leader to form a minority government. Churchill had crossed the floor at exactly the right time, as the next seventeen years would see Liberal Prime Ministers. Many of Churchills friends got senior government appointments, Edward Grey, Asquith, Haldane, John Morley, Lloyd George. Though Winston was only a newcomer, he too, was offered a government post, that of Financial Secretary at the Treasury. But though delighted to have his worth recognised, he decided not to accept that post. Instead he held out for Under-Secretary at the Colonial Office. His reasoning was that as the Minister sat in the Lords, his

Under-Secretary therefore would have full scope to handle business in the Commons and shine in the process. He was quite confident that he knew enough about the colonies to handle that portfolio. He got his wish.

The defeated Boers sent Jan Smuts to London to negotiate a final settlement with Churchill. What emerged was the virtual independence of Boer South Africa and within three years a united and stable country, under Smuts and Louis Botha. The Tories hated Churchill for giving away so much to the defeated Boers.

A General Election occurred shortly and Churchill had to go north to Manchester to face his new electorate. His was no easy constituency, complicated as it was by many groups and issues. There was a large Jewish vote; the Suffragette Movement was involved; there was a sizable Irish vote and the proximity to his previous Oldham constituency, all complicated the vote. Churchill decided he would keep quiet about his opposition to Irish Home Rule, though the Liberal Party had already promised not to introduce it in the next Parliament. He won the seat.

At about this time Churchill published the one thousand page biography of his father. This remained a story riven with bitter memories for many, but another step in paying off the debt Winston felt he owed Randolph. His literary agent, who secured a very successful contract for the book, was Frank Harris, who later became infamous for his own book - My Life and Loves. The book was very well received. One of the many letters he received about the book was from Wilfred Blunt, who wrote to him about his father's real attitude to Home Rule for Ireland. Winston and most people who recalled Randolph's rebellious call in Belfast to his fellow Tory-Unionists, that "Ulster Will fight and Ulster will be right", believed that the rhetoric mirrored his real attitudes. Blunt wrote of Randolph:

"He was far more of a Home Ruler than you seem to know, and I have always thought that, if the election of 1885 had gone rather more favourably and Gladstone had not taken up the Irish cause when he did, your father would have persevered with it". In 1908 Herbert Asquith succeeded Campbell-Bannerman as P.M. In the new Government Winston was promoted to full cabinet rank at the Board of Trade. But before he could settle down at that ministry, he had to vacate his seat at Manchester and fight a by election there. This procedure was a legacy of the Regency Act 1767, which forced new ministers to seek a fresh public mandate. The purpose of the Act had been to limit the power of the Crown to give sinecures to favoured people. Sometimes the opposition did not oppose the incumbent and gave him an unopposed run. But there was little likelihood of the Tory-Unionists affording any such favours to their arch enemy. It was a bitterly fought by election with Winston believing the outcome would hinge on how the nine hundred Irish votes went. He persuaded Asquith to allow him to say that the Liberals would put the issue of Irish Home Rule before the people at the next General Election. This ploy led to an Ulster loyalist presence in the campaign. But Churchill was to hold fast to the principle of Irish Home Rule from this time on. Unluckily for him, the Irish vote was also being manipulated by the local Catholic Bishop of Salford. The bishop was unhappy by the governments refusal to subsidise denominational education sufficiently and he advised his flock to vote Tory. Winston blamed his defeat on this factor. The Tories were exhilarated by the victory over their enemy. But this defeat did not interrupt Churchill's ministerial career as he shortly won a safe Liberal seat in Dundee, which he held for the next fifteen years.

Winston found life at the cabinet table to be a fascinating form of intrigue and manipulation. He came to admire Lloyd

George as the master of infighting and most importantly of getting things done. Many ministers confined their interests to their own brief and had no interest in getting involved in wider issues of cabinet responsibility. Others took a broader view and meddled regularly in other departmental issues, making alliances which shifted as the issues did. Winston was definitely of the latter mode.

A LADIES MAN

Winston had had several lady friends as a young man and might have married had his financial circumstances been more stable. Pamela Plowden, Helen Botha (daughter of Louis'), and the actress Ethel Barrymore were a few. For many men in his circumstances a marriage to a wealthy heiress would have been an obvious course. Then in 1908 at a dinner party, he met a young beauty named, Clementine Hozier. She, like him, was not wealthy and also had an unhappy childhood. She was unknown, but a Liberal and an intelligent person. He proposed to her in a Greek temple in the rose garden of Salisbury Hall and she accepted. They were married at St. Margaret's Westminster, the parish church of the House of Commons. He was thirty four and she twenty three. Among the guests were Sir Bindon Blood and Lloyd George. The King sent his congratulations. For their honeymoon they travelled to the beautiful Lake Lugano in northern Italy and then on to Venice. Winston wrote to his mother about their beautiful lovemaking. Back home they settled into a house in Eccleston Square near the Commons. Clementine had been used to fairly frugal living. She encouraged her husband to cut expenditure on cigars and clothes. She was shocked to discover that not alone did he gamble but that his mother also did. She took some time to merge into his upperclass style of living which did not expect any personal discomfort to intrude. Their love for each other carried them through many early difficulties. She became pregnant early in their marriage which helped her enormously to have a life of her own, when Winston was away from home.

CHAPTER 4

LET ULSTER FIGHT FOR THE HONOUR AND DIGNITY OF IRELAND

In Cabinet Winston and Lloyd George often became allies. They both were endeavouring to create employment and better working conditions for the ordinary worker. Churchill often antagonised his cabinet colleagues. Augustine Birrell, Chief Secretary for Ireland, believed that Winston always considered the ' rhetorical potentialities of any policy'. Birrell added that the cabinet, "are very forbearing to his chatter". Asquith said of him, "he thinks with his mouth". Sir Edward Grey said, "very soon Winston will become incapable from sheer activity of mind, of being anything in a cabinet but P.M.". At the Board of Trade Winston was able to become involved in social legislation. He said that:

"Modern industry is national. The facilities of transport and communication knit the country together, as no country has ever been knitted before. Labour alone, has not profited by this improved organisation. The method by which Labour obtains its market today is the old method, the demoralizing method of personal application, hawking Labour about from place to place, and treating a job as if it were a favour, as a thing which places a man under an obligation when he has got it".

In the ' People's Budget' of the same year Winston seconded Lloyd George's proposals, which sought to take some wealth from the rich and redistribute it among the poor. The Commons debated the Budget for seven months. It was a measure against the privilege of Churchill's own class and caused great family embarrassment. The House of Lords threatened to block the measure if passed in the Commons. Winston said if this occurred, a constitutional crisis would develop, and the government would dissolve Parliament. He had spoken without cabinet clearance and was chided by Asquith for, "purporting to speak on behalf of the Government" which was, "quite indefensible and altogether inconsistent with Cabinet responsibility and Ministerial cohesion". The Lords did vote the Budget down and Asquith dissolved Parliament. The General Election which followed resulted in a tie: the Tory-Unionist Conservatives got 273 seats to the Liberals 275. The Labour Party got 41 seats and the Irish Party 71. The Liberals then depended on the support of the Irish Party to remain in Government. The Irish Party had its own agenda of course which included Reform of the Lords and Home Rule for Ireland. The new Government decided to try to reform the Lords by creating more Peers favourable to them, unless the Lords passed government business.

Asquith offered Churchill the post of Chief Secretary for Ireland. If an Irish Home Rule Bill was ready, Churchill might have considered the offer, as it would have afforded him an opportunity to shine in the Commons. But he declined and sought a more prestigious post from Asquith. He now achieved senior cabinet rank with the post of Home Secretary.

THE IRISH PARLIAMENTARY PARTY DEMANDS

The Parliamentary situation was still one of crisis. The King refused to appoint extra government peers. The Irish Party pushed for this measure as well as for the introduction of

Home Rule, as the price for their support of the ' Peoples Budget'. The Irish Party proposed that the government should get the Lords to agree to end their veto on legislation. Churchill's strategy was to pass the budget first in the Commons and then let it go to the Lords. He found the Irish attitude, ' had something of a Hibernian flavour about it'. To which, John Redmond, the leader of the Irish Party retorted, "None the worst for that". Tim Healy of the same Party added to Churchill, "Have your taxes a Hibernian flavour? Will you refuse them on that account ?". Herbert Asquith succeeded in getting the Irish Party to support the budget, after promising that the Lords veto would be ended by withdrawing their power to veto any bill which was passed, on three successive sessions of the House of Commons. Asquith also gave the King an ultimatum on the Lords position. The budget was passed in April by the Commons. and the Lords acquiesced. Lloyd George and Churchill were heroes.

The Parliament Bill, to curb the Lords was introduced. Old King Edward who had opposed it had been succeeded by George V. The politicians were loath to have to ask him to begin his reign by creating hundreds of new peers. A Constitutional Conference was held and the possibility of a Coalition Government was mooted, as a way of breaking the deadlock. Lists of possible Coalition cabinets were being circulated. When Winston discovered that these generally omitted his name, he went in great anger to Lloyd George the arch manipulator saying, "You can go to hell in your own way. I won't interfere. I'll have nothing to do with your damned policy". The Conference made no progress. Asquith promised to force the King to agree to create the necessary extra peers, if he won the next General Election in November. The resulting Election saw a similar result as previously with the Irish Party holding the balance of power. Again they supported the Liberal Government.

The Parliament Bill passed in the Commons. The Lords sent it back completely decimated in power. Ferocious lobbying went on. Finally the King agreed to create the extra peers, if necessary. But in a climbdown by the Lords, when the Bill was returned to them, it was passed by 131 votes to 114. Their power was almost ended. The way was open to introduce an Irish Home Rule Bill in the next session of Parliament, where at worst the Lords could only delay the measure.

This Bill also introduced a payment for members of Parliament for the first time. They would now be paid £400 per annum. Up to this the position was considered only suitable for a gentleman, who had other income.

The Tory-Unionist-Conservative Party was furious to see the right of privilege, their privilege, ended. Their reaction was to turn on their own leader, Balfour, and depose him. They selected a dour teetotaller Presbyterian, named Andrew Bonar Law as their new leader.

THE SYDNEY STREET INCIDENT

Churchill had won much popular support for his work in Parliament on behalf of working people. But his period as Home Secretary was marred by two events which threw question marks on his true commitment to civil rights for all. The first such incident occurred at Sydney St. in London. An armed gang had shot dead three policemen. The gang was reputed to be part of a Latvian colony of anarchists, led by a man nicknamed, 'Peter the Painter'. Some weeks later, the Home Office was informed that the same gang were surrounded by the police at a house on Sydney St. Churchill authorised the police to use automatic revolvers and to call out twenty Scots Guards with rifles. The Horse Artillery also brought out canon guns. Winston went to the scene himself. The security forces were unable to dislodge the gunmen so they raised the house with fire until it went ablaze. When the fire brigade arrived, Churchill refused to let it put out the fire. An onlooker at the scene was Clement Attlee, then a social worker. When the fire eventually burned itself out, two bodies were found inside, neither of which was Peter the Painter. The episode was regarded as a blundering fiasco. Churchill was roundly criticised in Parliament and the press for actually going to the scene himself and for his actions there, particularly the calling out of troops. Winston defended himself to Charles Masterman, saying, "it was such fun". Major John MacBride, then in Dublin, commented, "It once again proclaims to the world the grotesque incapacity of the forces of the Empire, to tackle even so simple a proposition as the arrest of two individuals, without covering themselves and their nation in ridicule".

Later that same year of 1910, Churchill was confronted with great labour unrest in Tonypandy in the Rhonda Valley of Wales. He got General Sir Neville MacReady seconded to the Home Office, to assist the police with soldiers against the rioting strikers. Keir Hardie, the Labour leader blamed Churchill for, "letting loose troops upon the people to shoot down, if need be, whilst they are fighting for their legitimate rights".

Winston defended his actions in the Commons in February 1911 saying, "For soldiers to fire on the people would be a catastrophe in our national life. Alone among the nations,or almost alone, we have avoided for a great many years that melancholy and unnatural experience. And it is well worth while, I venture to think, for the Minister who is responsible to run some risk of broken heads or broken windows...to accept direct responsibility in order that the shedding of British blood by British soldiers may be averted as, thank god, it has been successfully averted in South Wales".

HOME RULE ALL- ROUND MANOEUVRES

After the Lords had been neutered, Churchill realised that the next major battle in the Commons would be on Irish Home Rule. In the summer of 1910 He had asked the Irish Party leader, John Redmond, to have a selection of books on Ireland sent to him. Redmond wrote to him saying, "all of us are counting on you to put Home Rule through". A cabinet sub committee had been set up to discuss the subject. Winston put foward the notion of Home Rule all round, which would create ten regional parliaments in the U.K. He submitted two papers on the matter to cabinet. It decided this was not a practical proposition, though it drew support from Scottish and Welsh nationalists. Asquith admitted that the proposed Irish Bill could be a model for the future. This federal idea also left open a possible solution, should Ulster again prove to be recalcitrant. In an editorial the Times noted that under such a scheme, two parliaments could be set up in Ireland, if necessary. Winston became Chairman of the Home Rule Council, which was to ensure that the government's plan would be adequately supported and funded. He urged Asquith to bring in the Bill.

The greatest opposition to Irish Home Rule would come from those Tory-Unionists in Ireland, who wanted to remain as part of the U.K., on the same basis as mainland Great Britain. Most of these had a vested interest in this, none more so than the Ulster Unionists, who believed that their future would be imperilled by a Dublin Parliament. In 1886, Gladstone's first Home Rule Bill made no mention of Ulster, although the

Unionists then, abetted by Randolph Churchill, had protested vehemently and threathened to resist it by force of arms.

Winston was very mindful of his father's role in Ulster, but he also remembered what Wilfred Blunt, a good friend of the Hozier and Churchill families, had written him on the matter. Winston was firmly behind Home Rule, as a government measure. He wanted to test the water in Ulster itself and decided to speak there in February 1912. The Ulster Liberal Association organised a meeting for the Ulster Hall. John Redmond was to share the platform with Churchill, but the latter wrote to Redmond saying, though he would very much like to speak with him, he doubted that a, 'joint appearance will really conduce to the public advantage'. The news of Churchill's impending visit began to create furore. The Ulster Unionists vowed to occupy the Ulster Hall and forbid him the right to speak there. This made him all the more determined to travel to Belfast. He wrote to Lord Londonderry, a family friend, though a Unionist: "No more crude assertion could be made of a claim to ascendancy than an open declaration by the Ulster Conservatives, that they will not allow their fellow-countrymen, from whom they differ, the right of public meeting". He added in a later letter to the same man, on the Unionist claim to the memory of his father Randolph's famous Ulster speech: "The Unionist party, who within a few months of the very speech which is now on their lips, pursued him with harsh ingratitude, have no such right". The row about the visit grew. The Irish Secretary, Birrell, wrote a testy letter to Winston, saying that he should have been consulted about the matter. He said that the idea that there could be disorder between the Protestants of Belfast and soldiers, was absurd. "In Belfast, two mobs are necessary - a Catholic mob and a Protestant mob - it is they who fight, and it is the military who seek to prevent them murdering each other". Birrell added that in future, Churchilll should leave Ireland alone.

CELTIC PARK WEST BELFAST

Eventually, a huge tent from Scotland, was erected on the Celtic Park football ground in Catholic West Belfast and the meeting went ahead there. Clementine insisted on travelling with her husband, thinking it would help to cool passions. But they were jostled and shouted at en route, by the Protestants, but were welcomed on the Falls Road, by the Catholics. The only interruptions at the meeting came from the Suffragettes, who always barricked Churchill. Winston finished his speech by saying: "Let Ulster fight for the dignity and honour of Ireland. Let her fight for the reconcilation of races and forgiveness of ancient wrongs. Let her fight for the unity and consolidation of the British Empire. Let her fight for the spreading of charity, tolerance and enlightenment among men. Then indeed, Ulster will fight and Ulster will be right". He had experienced the sectarian differences and measured the difficulties which lay ahead.

In the preparation of the Home Rule Bill, both Churchill and lloyd George, asked for the exclusion of Ulster. They questioned whether force would be used. They were told it was a possibility. The cabinet decided to let the Bill refer to all of Ireland. This was a tactical mistake, as it handed a major weapon to the Conservative - Unionists. Though at that same time, Asquith was telling the king that, "if it becomes clear that some special treatment must be provided for the Ulster counties, the Government will be ready to recognise the necessity". Though the measure was a major government issue, many of the cabinet had little interest or time for the Irish question. The three, apart from Asquith, who were interested were, Birrell, Lloyd George and Churchill. Birrell surprisingly had great difficulty in assessing whether the threat of violence in Ulster was real or bluff.

During the Second Reading of the Bill, Churchill broke cabinet ranks when he said: "the perfectly genuine apprehensions" of the Ulster Protestants were serious. He asked if the four Protestant counties of north east Ulster, looked for a Parliament of their own or wanted to remain under London? Either option would be disastrous for Ireland, he said. But he declared that the Protestants had no right to oppose Home Rule for the rest of Ireland. He said: "Half a province cannot impose a permanent veto on the nation. At one sweep of the hand, the Ulsterman could sweep the Irish question out of life and into history, and free the British realm of the canker, which poisoned its heart for generations. If they refuse, if they take to the boats, all we say is that they shall not obstruct the work of salvage, and we shall go foward at any rate to the end". Accusing Bonar Law and the Ulster Unionist leader, Sir Edward Carson, of "almost treasonable activity", he asked, "had British statesmen and leaders of great parties in the past allowed their thoughts so lightly to turn to projects of bloodshed, within the bosom of the country, we should have shared the follies of Poland".

Ulster was a geographical entity composed of nine counties. It was neither an administrative nor a political unit, though each county had a local administration and formed an electoral district. Nevertheless it was within this area that the Protestant Unionist Herrenvolk intended to protect their own identity and future. The total population of Ulster was about one and a half million people, of which 900,000 were Protestants and 700,000 Catholic Nationalists. But within the individual nine Ulster counties there were wide majority fluctuations. As Churchill indicated above, the Protestants were only in a majority in four counties. The 1911 Census showed:

County	Protestants (%)	Catholics (%)
Antrim	79.5	20.5
Down	68.4	31.6
Armagh	54.7	45.3
Londonderry	54.2	45.8
Tyrone	44.6	55.4
Fermanagh	43.8	56.2
Monaghan	25.3	74.7
Donegal	21.1	78.9
Cavan	18.5	81.5

Though harshly critical, Churchill's speech was clearly a phillip for the Unionists of Ulster, as it recognised their position and power. Nevertheless, Lloyd George spoke trenchantly for the Bill as it stood, saying that the cabinet was behind it. The Second Reading was carried by 320 votes to 251, with much split voting noted.

Both Lloyd George and Churchill wished to get the Home Rule Bill out of the way and concentrate on much needed social legislation. They were also concerned about the possibility of a war against Germany. Winston had left the Home Office and was at the Admiralty since September 1911. That Department had many pressing problems to attend to, especially on the provision of extra monies for the navy. After getting this Ministry he commented to Asquith's daughter, Violet in high glee; "Look at the people I have had to deal with so far - judges and convicts. This is a big thing - the biggest thing that has ever come my way".

TAKES UP FLYING

He became very interested in the possibilities of aviation for the army and navy. He took up flying himself, frightening his family and flying instructors. The latter were most reluctant to go up with him, least an accident occur and they be blamed. He lacked basic timing and coordination, which had made him such a terrible car driver that even his wife was most reluctant to motor with him. After several fatal air accidents, Winston decided to give up his flying on a temporary basis.

ULSTER THREATENS VIOLENCE

Winston was shocked to find the Conservative leaders so openly threatening violence on Ulster. He wondered that they did not seem to consider what they would do, if returned to power, and be confronted with an ungovernerable Ireland. "They are the more inexcusable because no one that I know of, has ever contemplated the application of force to Ulster. The principle and doctrine lately enunciated would dissolve the framework, not only of the British Empire, but of civil society". Bonar Law had attended a march past of 80,000 men in Belfast opposed to Home Rule. He and Edward Carson had seen 13,000 men march past them at Blenheim, where Carson said they would resist Home Rule by force. Bonar Law had said; "I do not anticipate civil war...There would have been a real danger of civil war, if the government had been allowed to move blindly towards the precipice, without a clear warning of the dangers in front of them". Churchill quoted this statement in writing to the President of the Dundee Liberal Association, adding, "His (Bonar Law) colleague, Sir Edward Carson is the moving spirit in an organisation which has openly avowed its intention to set up a provisional government, i.e., a government against the Crown and Parliament of these realms. There has been a large importation of arms, into the Orange counties of Ulster: there is widespread drilling and training in the use of lethal weapons". Churchill also quoted Bonar Law as saying at Blenheim: "There is no length to which the people of Ulster may go in which, I shall not support them. The government was a revolutionary committee which has seized upon despotic power by fraud".

That same month of August Winston wrote to Lloyd George, urging some break in the logjam of Home Rule. He said: "The time has come when action about Ulster must be settled. We ought to give any Irish county the option of remaining at Westminster, for a period of five to ten years, or some variant of this. This ought to be settled one way or the other, with the Irish, before Parliament meets, and announced at the very beginning of the session, prior to or simultaneous with the guillotine motions. Time has in no way weakened the force of the arguments you used in January, and I am prepared to support you in pressing them". Churchill also wrote to John Redmond about this policy of exclusion. He felt that "the vital thing was to set up the Irish Parliament in Dublin, before the General Election. Once set up, it can never be cast down. The economic pressure which the rest of Ireland could gradually bring to bear on Belfast and the feeling of confidence which would be created, if the Irish Parliament was a dignified and successful body would, I believe, overcome the misgivings of the Orangemen, or, at any rate, of a majority in the Orange counties, in the course of a few years... I would also, if I had my way, at an early stage in the proceedings, take power to delay the operations of the Act, in regard to certain counties, where it was clear that the majority was opposed to it". Later at a party meeting in Dundee, Churchill once more decided to go public on Home Rule, by proposing ten federal legislatures, thus effectively opening the door to two Parliaments in Ireland. Again, he had spoken without cabinet knowledge or approval. Bonar Law immediately interpreted this as allowing Ulster a separate Parliament. In Ulster the Ulster Covenant was solemnly signed by thousands swearing to fight against incorporation into a Dublin Parliament.

Churchill wrote to J. Bait on the dangers to Protestants under Home Rule: There is not the slightest danger, in my opinion of Protestants in Ulster, being persecuted for their religion, under a system of Home Rule. The danger is entirely the other way, viz - that the very strong and aggresive Protestant majority in parts of north east Ulster, will maltreat and bully the Catholics in their midst. This had recently occurred on several occasions, and is in my opinion, the direct result of the encouragement given to bigotry and lawlessness by the leaders of the Conservative Party". The Prime Minister, Asquith, told Churchill that the King was obsessed by the Home Rule problem. He asked Churchill, who was going to see the King, to emphasise to him that, "an ungovernable Ireland is a much more serious prospect, than rioting in four counties". The Unionists put down an amendment to the Bill, looking for a nine county Ulster Exclusion. But this was rejected, with Winston speaking in the Commons for the government. The amendment was lost by 294 votes to 197. The third Reading passed by 369 votes to 257. Asquith refused an Ulster compromise, saying in Dublin: "Quite frankly, I do not believe in the prospect of civil war". He believed in the last analysis, Ulster patriots would not defy, "the supreme authority of the Imperial Parliament". Asquith therefore, had no plans to deal with any Ulster rebellion. In 1913, the Commons passed the Home Rule Bill, the Lords rejected it, the Commons re-passed it, and the Lords rejected it again.

KING PROPOSES CONSTITUTIONAL CONFERENCE

Bonar Law threatened organised disorder of the Commons. The King got more uneasy. Churchill met Bonar Law at Balmoral where the King put forward the idea of a Constitutional Conference. Bonar Law told Churchill that Carson would take over Ulster, if Home Rule became law. Churchill emphasised to Bonar Law during a game of golf, that as Britishers, they should be able to solve the Irish problem. Balfour, who was also at Balmoral, felt that it was wrong to exclude any from the Union, who did not wish for it. Churchill set up meetings between Bonar Law and Asquith, but the furthest Asquith would go, was to offer some temporary exclusion to part of Ulster. Bonar Law had also mentioned to Churchill the possibility that the Unionists, might urge army officers to ignore government orders to use force against Ulster.

Asquith later wrote to Churchill saying; "I always thought (and said) that, in the end, we should probably have to make some sort of bargain about Ulster, as the price of Home Rule. But I have never doubted, that, as a matter of tactics and policy, we were right to launch our Bill on its present lines". T.P. O'Connor, journalist and Irish Party member, wrote to Churchill that the Irish, "are irreconcilably hostile to any break up of Ireland. I believe that they would positively prefer a postponement of Home Rule, for some years, rather than consent to such a mutilation of the country. This is not the time for a conference. The Tories would lay down impossible terms". Winston continued to be the go between for the various parties. He saw Bonar Law and Balfour again and told them that he felt, "the nationalists could be made to agree to the exclusion of Ulster" and that he had some cabinet agreement to this. Carson told Bonar Law that his minimum insistence was for six counties. On 8 October, Churchill speaking at Dundee said: "Our Bill is not unalterable and the procedure of the Parliament Act, renders far-reaching alterations possible. But only on one condition - There must be agreement". John Redmond immediately condemned the speech and Ulster exclusion as, "totally impracticable". John Dillon, Irish Party M.P., said, "the whole idea of lopping off part of Ireland, is quite unworkable and so grotesque, that I am sure, the Government will never dream of it".

Churchill wanted to treat Ulster fairly, but he also wanted to give it a lesson on the threats to use force against the government. At cabinet in October he pleaded, "not to close the doors to a temporary exclusion of the homogenous anti-national part of Ulster, and that if we could avert a crisis by exempting Ulster for five years, we ought to do it, but only if Carson and the Tory Party, would accept the compromise and agree not to repeal it". But a week later, in a tactical move, he said at Manchester, that he was happy with," fair and honourable proposals accepting the unity of Ireland and the establishment of an Irish Parliament". At the same time, he had asked T.P. O'Connor to consider the proposal to exclude four counties, on a temporary basis. He was acting as a British politican trying to solve the intractable Irish problem and keeping all options open.

CHAPTER 5

APPEASING THE UNIONISTS

The Irish question was driving deep divisions within British society. Bitter antipathy had developed over the sidelining of the House of Lords. The Peoples Budget had set a precedent for taking from the wealthy. The Liberals were seen as radicals, who were out to change society from being well ordered and civilised, to one where crudity and vulgarity prevailed. Worst of all, the Irish Bill was threatening to destroy the country and bring constitutional chaos and civil disorder. The Prime Minister Asquith took most of the blame, with his Chancellor of the Exchequer, Lloyd George, not far behind. The old enemy of the Tories, Winston Churchill, had long since betrayed his forebears, but even he was made to feel uncomfortable, as was his wife on social occasions. But he was the prima donna of the Liberal party, and though thoughts of reverting to the Tories sometimes crossed his mind, he contented himself, with being a bridge between the parties, while at the same time vigorously pursuing government policy.

At the Admiralty, he was in close contact with the Germans and saw a war looming as their navy was gradually put on a war footing. Meanwhile, he had to fight desperately, in cabinet, to get the necessary finance to keep up with them. Much of the wheeling and dealing on government business took place at dinner tables. Lloyd George held one such dinner party in November 1913, at the instigation of Churchill, to try to sort out government policy on Ireland. He felt that they had to plan a strategy and stick to it. All the leading cabinet members were at the dinner, including Asquith. Lloyd George's plan was to, 'knock all moral props from under Carson's rebellion and either make it impossible for Ulster to take up arms, or if they did, put us in a strong position with British public opinion, when we come to suppress it'. He therefore suggested a temporary exclusion of Ulster, with an automatic inclusion at the end of the term. This scheme met with general approval - no objections were raised to it. There was no public declaration of the new policy and at Leeds two weeks later. Asquith spoke at length saying he intended "to see this thing through". Churchill kept in touch with Bonar Law and Joseph Chamberlain. Asquith saw Carson and demanded that he should at least present in black and white some suggested method, by which " veiled exclusion could be put into effect, without mutilating the Home Rule scheme as a whole and hopelessly offending nationalist sentiment". Asquith threatened the Irish Party that the government would fall, by government resignation, including that of Churchills, unless they agreed to the plan.

At this time in cabinet, there was a furious row going on over naval estimates, with Churchill and Lloyd George, on opposite sides. Churchill wanted more money for naval expansion and the Chancellor was resisting him. The threat of resignations were in the air. Some ministers suspected that Churchill was seeking to create an opportunity for himself to resign, over the estimates or Irish Home Rule. Both men had been dubbed the 'Heavenly Twins', but now there was deadlock. The Liberal Party wished to spend money on social measures and not on a war machine. Churchill announced that he would resign unless he got money for at least four new ships. He chided Lloyd

George that he had previously promised him support. He said he would bring down the government on the issue. He believed that the British navy had to maintain a certain level of superiority over the Germans to avert a war. The cabinet continued to be split on the matter as they went into 1914. Finally Lloyd George capitulated, deciding for whatever reasons, possibly for Churchill's support for Home Rule, that the Admiralty should have its ships. Winston had won.

Introducing the Estimates in the Commons Winston said: "These are the largest estimates ever presented to this House, but I hope the House will not think it necessary on that account that I should introduce them in the longest speech ever delivered".

The victory did not make Winston popular in the Liberal party, where sentiment was decidedly against increase in naval expenditure. He then took a deliberate decision to get more immersed in trying to bring the party policy on Home Rule to fruition.He wrote, "In order to strengthen myself with my party, I mingled actively in the Irish controversy. In the Commons he said on Home Rule:

"I was wounded and grieved deeply to find this offer,on which so many of us had pinned our hopes, was so unceremoniously rejected and repulsed". As it was clear that the Home Rule Bill would be passed for the third time that parliamentary session, and thus become law, the dye was cast. In Ulster, the Protestants, with the blessing of their fellow Tories in Britain, continued to prepare for armed resistance. The King became desperate at the crisis, suggesting to Asquith that army officers would resign rather than fight in Ulster. The King suggested the holding of a General Election on the matter. Asquith then, formally proposed an amendment to the Bill, excluding Ulster for six years. Carson rejected this, describing it as, "a stay of execution for six years". John Redmond said his party would consider the amendment.

Asquith had adopted Lloyd George's earlier proposals for a six year exclusion. Churchill congratulated Lloyd George, "This is a great triumph for your diplomacy". John Redmond felt that the Irish Nationalists had to agree saying, "We feel we cannot refuse an extension of five years". Asquith and Carson believed that the four north east counties of Ulster would vote for exclusion. Bonar Law believed that six counties should be excluded for six years and then a local referendum be held to see if they wished to remain excluded. John Redmond rejected the suggestion of a referendum.

CABINET'S BLUFF IS CALLED

The Cabinet was only belatedly told of the dangerous situation in Ulster, where it was feared, that the Ulster Volunteers might take control of military targets and arms stores. A cabinet sub committee was formed to coordinate the British military response to the Ulster Volunteers. Churchill sat on this committee. He was also encouraged to make a major speech on the issue, as one who would be listened to. Lloyd George said, "You can make a speech that will ring down the corridors of history. I could not do it. You are the only member of the cabinet who could make such a speech. You are known to have been in favour of conciliation for Ulster. Now you can say that having secured a compromise, Ulstermen will have to accept it or take the consequences".

In March, Churchill went to St. Georges Hall in Bradford to address a crowd of three thousand, on Irish Home Rule policy. He spoke of the governments offer to the Protestants of Ulster that gave any county the power to vote itself out of the Bill for a six year period. He went on: "But if there is no wish for peace, if every concession that is made is spurned and exploited... if all the loose and wanton and reckless chatter, we have been forced to listen to all these many months, is in the end to disclose a sinister and revolutionary purpose: there are worse things than bloodshed — then gentlemen I can only say to you, let us go forward together and put these grave matters to the proof".

This declaration sounded bellicose and was read as such by the Tories and their Ulster Protestant allies. Liberals applauded it. The cabinet committee on Ireland decided that it had to take steps to safeguard military installations in Ulster, which were in danger. Churchill offered to use the navy to assist in the operation. He ordered several warships to proceed towards Ulster. The cabinet had received alarming reports that 80,000 Ulster Volunteers had acquired 17,000 rifles and planned to seize military installations. The committee considered whether they should arrest Carson. The Irish Secretary, Birrell, put it to the cabinet; "can he be allowed to preach and practise sedition and mutiny, right up to the passage of the Bill ?". The Irish Party advised not to arrest Carson and this was the cabinet decision. Instead they decided to move troops into Ulster from southern Ireland and from Great Britain, by sea.

General Jack Seely, who like Churchill had crossed the floor of the Commons to join the Liberals, was the Secretary for War. He summoned General Paget, officer commanding in Ireland, to London. He instructed him to organise the deployment of the troops northward. Paget warned that many officers had pro Ulster views. He mentioned how Field Marshal Lord Roberts himself, had signed the Ulster Covenant. Seely told Paget verbally that he should discuss the operation with his senior officers. Those officers who did not obey orders should be dismissed. But those who had Ulster sympathies could be sent on leave or could resign their commissions. At the Curragh, the military headquarters in Ireland, fifty- eight officers including General Gough, opted to resign their commissions. Gough was called to London, where it transpired that no order had been given to go north and none had refused a command. It had all been hypothetical. Gough and the other officers were reinstated. But the angry Gough, demanded it be put in writing, that the army would not be used to coerce Ulster into Home Rule. A note was produced which was a fudge of the matter. Gough was furious. Seely then on his own initiative, added a clear message, to the effect that the government had the right to use the army to exercise law and order, "but they have no intention whatever, of taking advantage of this right, to crush political opposition to the policy and principle of the Home Rule Bill". General French and Ewart, signed this statement for the Army Council, on Seely's instructions, assuming that it had been agreed in cabinet.

This debacle, with the army effectively refusing government authority, soon became public knowledge. Asquith told Churchill to put his naval movements (taken on his own initiative) on hold, while they considered the crisis with the army. In the Commons Asquith had to say that Seely had acted without authority, and that the government were not bound by his statement to General Gough. Seely, French and Ewart had to resign. But it was clear for all to see that a major impediment in the implementation of government policy, had been encountered in what has been rightly called - the Curragh Mutiny. Where there was even a doubt about the army's response to government instructions, then that government was severally wounded. In the Commons Churchill defended the planned military movements saying they were: "The first step in an insidious but deeply laid strategic scheme, for grasping the vital key positions for a general advance on Ulster...So extraordinary is the position we have reached that the doctrine is seriously put forward, that the only force which is legitimate to use is rebellious force...But against armed rebellion, if it occurs, force is certainly justified". The government was assailed by the Tory - Unionists as planning an assault on Ulster and splitting the loyalty of the army. They accused Churchill of planning an ' Ulster Pogrom', particularly when details of the navys involvement with gunships, was made public. He was vilified by Bonar Law and Carson. Lord Beresford wrote to Rear Admiral Rosslyn Wemyss, "Churchill ought to be hanged". Carson called him, "Randolphs renegade son" and "the Belfast butcher".

DOMESTIC CHORES

Winston wrote to his wife, who was away from London, showing that though he discussed political events with her, they did not completely occupy his mind: "The 'Ulster Pogrom' is in full swing...The kittens are extremely well and make continuous enquiries and complaints about your non-return... Our finances are in a condition which requires serious and prompt attention. The expenses of the first quarter of 1914, with our holiday trip, is quite astonishing. Money seems to be flowing away. Fondest love my darling and many kisses from the babes and me. Always your loving and devoted husband. W.".

The pressure on the government eased somewhat, when during the night of 24 April, 35,000 rifles and three million bullets were landed at Larne in county Antrim, near Belfast, by the Ulster Volunteers. Churchill spoke on a vote of censure on the government, by Austin Chamberlain in the Commons; "What we are now witnessing in this House is uncommonly like a vote of censure by the criminal class on the police. It was a question of preventing Ulster from coercing us...All of this talk of civil war has not come from us; it has come from you. For the last two years we have been forced to listen to a drone of threats of civil war, with the most blood-curdling accompaniments and consequences. Did they really think that if a civil war came, it was to be a war in which only one side was to take action ?... I wish to make it perfectly clear that if rebellion comes, we shall put it down". But Churchill ended his speech in an almost contradictory fashion by being most conciliatory to Carson, saying that he understood the need for Ulster to have safeguards. He urged Carson to accept the six year exclusion amendment. This tone of Churchills, surprised his party and made them suspect his motives, especially when Carson replied in a conciliatory way too. The Irish Party were furious with this development, with J.G. Devlin saying Churchill had betrayed the Irish cause. Many Liberals feared the breakup of the government. Winston himself realised the seriousness of the situation. He wrote to his wife on 29 April, saying he had taken a major risk: "I took my political life in my hands. The Irish are very restive and there is danger everywhere". He was advised, "that unless the Prime Minister states unmistakably, that your offer was not the decision of the cabinet, there is a definite danger of an open rupture". Churchill himself knew what he was doing. He was quite prepared for a war. But he wanted a settlement, if at all possible, and the Ulster Unionists read that clearly. It left them in a stronger tactical position. Churchills own cabinet partners also read that situation, and were infuriated with him.

Ted Morgan writes: "His policy was one of appeasement, from a position of strength. But with the army divided, and the two political parties at each others throats, was it surprising that German agents reported that England was drifting into civil war, and was so preoccupied by the Irish problem, that it was no longer a factor in the European situation".

The Ulster Unionists responded by reopening the possibility of an all round Federal Devolution. Churchill greeted this development enthusiastically, which deepened suspicions. But the idea found little or no backing in the Commons. On the Second Reading of the Bill the idea of a National Referendum was defeated and the six year exclusion term was not extended. The third Reading passed unamended on 25 May. When the Bill went to the Lords, they dropped the six year time limit and voted for a permanent exclusion of all nine Ulster counties. This would mean little, if the Commons held fast. The Liberal Chief Whip issued a message to all party members on 13 July saying: "The time has arrived for a sustained effort and with everything at stake for which generations of Liberals have laboured, I am relying on your constant attendance and support for the remainder of the session".

EVENTS AT SARAJEVO IMPINGE ON HOME RULE

The King, fearful of the dire consequences of civil war, convened an all party conference at Buckingham Palace. On 22 July Churchill wrote to the Foreign Secretary, Sir Edward Grey: "The conference should labour to reduce the differences to the smallest definite limits possible. At that point, if no agreement had been reached, the Speaker should be asked to propose a partition; and we should urge the Unionist leaders to accept it. It is only when this or some such proposal has been made or refused, that I should be prepared to look for the, no doubt, good tactical positions you indicate. I do not want good tactical positions for war. I want peace by splitting the outstanding differences, if possible, with Irish acquiescence, but if necessary over the heads of both Irish parties". That same day he wrote to his wife: "The conference is in extremus. We are preparing a partition of Tyrone with reluctant nationalist acquiescence. Carson absolutely refuses, although the speaker strongly commended it. Carson and Redmond both just friendly and apparently not hopeless. But what about us - 40 millions!". Two days later the conference broke down and the P.M. reported to the cabinet. This same cabinet meeting heard that the Austrian government had issued an ultimatum to Serbia, resulting from the murder of the Archduke Ferdinand, four weeks earlier at Sarajevo. Churchill later wrote of that moment: "The parishes of Fermanagh and Tyrone faded back into the mists and squalls of Ireland, and a strange light began immediately, but by imperceptible gradations, to fall upon the map of Europe".

Three days later, he cancelled the naval movements connected with Ireland and put the entire navy on maximum alert for war.

The Second Reading of the Amendment Bill to the Home Rule measure was due to be taken on 30 July. But this was postponed due to the impending war. John Redmond lobbied Asquith and Churchill for the enactment of the Home Rule Bill. He told Churchill on 4 August:"If the Bill be postponed (my people) will consider themselves sold and I will be simply unable to hold them. In that deplorable event, things will be said and done in Ireland and the Home Rule cause may be lost for our time". Redmond suggested that the Bill be given Royal assent with a promise that an amending Bill be introduced later, before the original Bill be made operative. He told Asquith that if the government allowed itself to be bullied by Carson, then the Irish Party would have to make difficulty on the Second Reading of the Appropriations Bill, which would have dire consequences for Ireland. Redmond intended to get Ireland behind the war effort and did not want to be exposed as being in dispute with the government. He said he did not believe in Carson's threats as public opinion in Britain was otherwise concerned then. He ended by saying: "This undoubtedly is the greatest opportunity that has ever occurred in the history of Ireland, to win the Irish people to loyalty to the Empire, and I do beg of you, not to allow threats of the kind used prevent you from taking the course which will enable me, to preach the doctrines of peace, goodwill and loyalty in Ireland".

In September the Home Rule Bill was put on the Statute Book. But The Act was suspended for one year, or until after the war. Asquith promised to introduce an amending Bill, dealing with Ulster exclusion. Bonar Law said Asquith had acted treacherously, just like the Kaiser had done by invading Belgium. He led his followers in a walk out of the Commons. Asquith was unperturbed, comparing it to," a lot of prosaic and for the most part, middle-aged gentlemen trying to look like French revolutionists in the Tennis Court". Clementine Churchill, who was in the House, was sickened by the display. Redmond accepted the compromise as the best he could get. The Ulster Unionists felt betrayed and only the war in Europe stopped them declaring unilateral independence. Meanwhile Winston was totally immersed by the European conflict with his mind gone from the intricacies of cabinet and parliamentary intrigue on Home Rule, as he wrote to his wife: "Everything tends towards catastrophe and collapse. I am interested, geared up and happy. Is it not horrible to be built like that? The preparations have a hideous fascination for me. I pray to god to forgive me for such fearful moods of levity. Yet I would do my best for peace and nothing could induce me wrongfully to strike the blow".

CHAPTER 6

AN UNHAPPY WAR FOR WINSTON

Early in 1915, when it was clear that the war would not end as quickly as some people had thought, Churchill was one of the people who mooted the idea of a national coalition government. Asquith and Lloyd George were against the idea. Bonar Law felt that the Tories could support the war effort more effectively outside the government. The Tory leaders were then invited to the War Council and received its papers. This was an opportunity for Winston to become friendly with them, especially Balfour, who began to frequent the Admiralty. This made Asquith suspicious.

The war became more complicated when Turkey joined the German alliance and the Germans mined the Dardanelles which controlled passage from the Black sea to the Mediterranean. It was vital that the Dardanelles be reopened. Churchill had been an advocate of the Dardanelles Strategy - which would bombard and take the Gallipoli Peninsula, reopen the waterway and take Constantinople. His old colleague, General Kitchener, no friend of Churchills and then head of the army, was supposed to back up the planned assault by the Navy, with a suitable military force. Asquith was completely behind the scheme. In the event the campaign proved a fiasco with shocking loss of young life, due to poor logistic and military backup. Asquith said publicly that there were no munition shortages, only to be contradicted in the

Times (14 May), by a Colonel Repington, who was in situ in Turkey. John Dillon M.P., wrote to Birrell: "The attack in yesterdays Times on the government and the statement by its military correspondent, on which the attack is based, is an unparalleled and amazing piece of blackguardism and treachery. How, I should like to know, did the censors pass this atrocious statement?... it is enough to bring down a government - and its publication must have that object in view". The Times of course was a Tory paper. Lord Fisher, First Lord of the Admiralty, who protested to Churchill, that he had always been against the Dardanelles Strategy, resigned his position. Churchill desperately tried to convince him otherwise as he knew such a move would leave himself completely exposed politically.

Asquith decided that it was essential to form a broader government and bring in the other parties. He saw Churchill and told him; "The whole nation is filled with gratitude for what you have done. I do not have to tell you of my admiration". Thus Winston heard of his own dismissal from the Admiralty. Birrell, the Irish secretary wrote, "My position is odd. They can't touch me. It is not the strength of the garrison, but the invulnerability of my position". So due to the niceties of Home Rule, Birrell was left untouched. The incoming Tories hated Churchill. The Liberal party was always highly suspicious of him. He had also been spoken of, as the person who inspired the Repington letter to the Times, which had precipitated the crisis.

The same Times wrote of his involvement in the Dardanelles, "when a civilian minister in charge of a fighting service persistently seeks to grasp power which should not pass into his unguided hands, and attempts to use that power in perilous ways, it is time for his colleagues in the cabinet to take some action. Such is the stage they appear to have reached". Clementine thought her husband would die of grief. Ironically, it was Balfour who got Churchills job. Chamberlain got the Indian Office with Bonar Law becoming Colonial Secretary. Edward Carson also joined the government, though the Irish Party declined office. Of the Ministers, twelve were Liberals, nine Tory-Unionist, one Labour and Lord Kitchener was a non party member. Though it had been Kitchener who had stood back and let the navy incur such a defeat at the Dardanelles, it was Churchill who got the opprobrium for the defeat. Kitchener had argued that he needed an army of three million men and that conscription was essential. Some Liberals had opposed this on expenditure grounds, but neither Churchill not Lloyd George had taken that position.

Winston was distraught to loose his Ministry. He berated Lloyd George that he did not care what happened to him. Clementine Churchill wrote to Asquith pleading with him not to dispense with her husband. In absolute desperation, Winston himself appealed to Bonar Law for help, but without success. Then he wrote to Asquith for a meeting. Asquith replied by letter telling Winston that his days at the Admiralty were ended, but that he hoped to retain him in the cabinet. He was given the post of Chancellor of the Duchy of Lancaster, the lowest office in cabinet, with no portfolio. It was a shocking comedown for such a man to have hardly any official duties and a war going on. He became depressed. He was obsessed with Gallipoli and the continuing campaign there. Lord Kitchener invited him to go to the Dardanelles to see the situation at first hand, but Bonar Law, outraged at such a suggestion, objected and Winston did not go. Sir Edward Carson resigned from the government over a lack of help to Serbia.

A Commission was set up in 1916 to consider what went wrong at the start of the Dardanelles campaign and specifically at Gallilpoli. Churchill was under a cloud until this report issued. It did not appear until 1917, all the while leaving Winston like a leper. When the Report did appear, it said that he should have consulted more widely with his experts before assenting "to an attack on the outer forces of the Dardanelles and to progressive operations thereafter up the Straits... Without in any way wishing to impugn his good faith it seems clear that he was carried away by his sanguine temperament". The Commission reached no conclusion on Gallipoli.

RESIGNS GOVERNMENT AND GOES TO WAR IN STYLE

A new war council, which did not include Churchill, was proclaimed on 11 November 1915. Winston announced his resignation from government the same day. He decided that he would rejoin his old army regiment, the Oxford Hussars, in France. As a boy his father had told him regularly that he was useless at everything except playing at soldiers. He had disproved that but now was happy to put his life at risk, haunted perhaps by the dreadful loss of life at Gallipoli, for he must have, felt some responsibility. As usual Winston went to war with some style. Among his baggage, which filled a whole taxicab, was a trunk full of assorted spirits, wines and good cigars. He kissed his wife and children goodbye and drove off dressed in his major's uniform. In France Sir John French welcomed him like an old friend, telling him that John Redmond had recently visited the front. Thousands of Irishmen had answered Redmond's call to join His Majesty's forces and were fighting on the continent. French asked Winston what he would like to do. He replied that he would do whatever he was ordered. He was offered the choice of remaining at Headquarters as an A.D.C. or joining the action. He chose the latter where he got a frosty reception from his fellow officers, who were highly suspicious of him and had not been consulted about his arrival. But gradually after his move to the trenches of the front line, they mellowed towards him. He was even appointed second in command by his officer commanding. The main action consisted of constant German shelling of the trenches. Winston enjoyed the danger and horror of it all. But as usual he did get special treatment as he was visited by a variety of notables like, Lord Curzon, Attorney General F.E. Smith, and General Jack Seely. Clementine sent him a pillow and food and drink. They wrote to each other almost daily. Clementine was thrilled, as was Winston, when he was to get command of a brigade. This later transpired to be a battalion of war weary infantrymen, the Sixth Royal Scots Fusiliers. He commanded them for about three months, during which 138 were killed in trench warfare.

In March 1916 a reorganisation in the army saw an amalgamation of the sixth and the seventh Scots battalions. As the colonel of the seventh was senior to Colonel Churchill, he would get the new command. Winston decided that this was an opportune time to leave the army and return to political life.

A fresh campaign of vilification of Churchill started in the press. The Daily Mail editorialised: "In the Dardanelles affair in particular a megalomaniac politician risked the fate of our army and sacrificed thousands of lives to no purpose". Churchill longed to see his name cleared by the Dardanelles Commission which had not yet began to sit.

Conscription was introduced as the cabinet squabbled. The Irish Party along with Labour opposed the measure. But the Irish rebellion at Easter 1916 shook the anti-conscriptionists. This rebellion led to the resignation of Birrell and the assumption of the Irish Office by the ailing Asquith. He toured Ireland in May as the army reacted with extreme force by executing the leaders of the rebellion. One of these was Major John MacBride of the Irish Brigade in the Boer War. Asquith wrote to his wife: "you never get to the bottom of this dark, perplexing and damnable country".

Asquith was dissuaded by his cabinet and a massive public campaign from extending conscription to Ireland. Sir Edward Carson was outraged by this decision. Later he and a group of sixty four Tory-Unionists, voted against the government on the question of confiscating enemy property. They were joined by about twelve Liberals, including Churchill. Their object was to oust Bonar Law, who was seen to be the main support behind the weakening Asquith. Lloyd George abstained on that vote. When Asquith did resign in December, Lloyd George became Prime Minister of the coalition government. Bonar Law got the Chancellorship, Balfour the Foreign Office and Carson the Admiralty. The old guard of Liberal ministers disappeared. Churchill was not promoted, mostly due to Conservative opposition. He "blazed with righteous anger". The problem for Lloyd George was that the Dardanelles Commission still had not reported, and until it did so, Churchill was untouchable. But Lloyd George did sent Winston a message saying that he would make him, Chairman of the Air Board, as soon as the Commission report was out of the way. This finally occurred in mid 1917, when Churchill was cleared of all serious charges and Kitchener got some of the blame for delaying army support. Winston was appointed Minister of Munitions. The Tories were outraged. The Morning Post called him: "the unsinkable politician...who had committed at least two capital blunders which cost the nation many thousands of lives and an appalling lost of prestige".

In March 1918 as the war cabinet were to begin a meeting at ten Downing St., Lloyd invited Churchill to attend. One of the matters under discussion was the extension of conscription to those aged fifty. They also discussed extending it to Ireland. Sir Henry Wilson, of the Army Office, was backing this measure and he got Churchill's support. But no decision was taken as the P.M. was very wary of such a move.

1918 ELECTION

The following month Winston was looking towards the future politically. He believed that the war cabinet was alright for conducting the war, but that, ' so narrow and unrepresentative a body ' should not settle the main policy of State. He felt that Lloyd George should form a political instrument for definite purposes, such as ' the passing of a Home Rule Bill for Ireland'. He was unhappy that ministers outside the war cabinet, like himself, might only be invited to attend at the whim of that group. He pointed out to the P.M. that all the main ministries were held by the Tories and that this would lead to losses for Liberal policy. Lloyd George did not take any of this advice and at the end of the war, only he, of the Liberal party, had been a member of the war cabinet. Five had been Tory, two Labour and one non-party. In the wider cabinet, the Tories had fourteen positions, the Liberals eight, and Labour two. The Liberals were very dissatisfied as a general election was called with the intention of maintaining the coalition government. Disgruntled Liberals looked to Asquith to lead a Liberal revival, but he and other Liberals opposed to the coalition fared badly. The total pro-coalition results were: Tories- 335; Liberals - 133; Labour - 10: 478 in all. Those opposed were; Labour - 63; Liberal - 28; Tories - 23; Irish Unionist - 25; Irish

Party - 7. A remaining 73 seats were won in Ireland by a new Party called, Sinn Fein, which had decided to abandon Westminster as a Parliamentary forum. Churchill asked, "Why do not the Irish leaders come forward now and take up the burden and responsibility of government within the British Empire?".

Winston had polled hugely in Dundee and was rewarded by Lloyd George as Secretary of State for the army and airforce. This drew the usual criticism from the Times, Morning Post and Daily Mail. His wife's major concern was that it gave him the impetus to take up flying again. He wrote, "the air is an extremely dangerous, jealous and exacting mistress. Once under the spell, most lovers are faithful to the end, which is not always old age...". Shortly afterwards he and his instructor were involved in a crash in which the latter broke both legs. Winston gave up flying.

Chapter 7

GET THREE GENERALS IF YOU CANNOT GET THREE JUDGES

The General Election of 1918 changed the politics of Ireland totally and had a major impact on Westminster also. The block of the old Irish Parliamentary Party members was decimated, and the only block vote now coming from Ireland was that of the Tory-Unionists. The Liberal Party lost an ally. In Ireland, the seeds sown by the rising at Easter 1916, came to fruition when Sinn Fein succeeded the Irish Party as the democratic representatives of the Irish people. Sinn Fein (Ourselves Alone) had been founded in 1905 at a convention in Dublin by Arthur Griffith. It was part of the Gaelic revival movement which got a major political phillip when Home Rule was not delivered. Efforts to introduce conscription also helped it. Sinn Fein was dedicated to setting up its own Parliament in Dublin, no longer asking for that right from the imperial parliament, but ready to take it. The old idea of Home Rule was also rejected. The move now was for full independence.

On 15 January 1919, the elected Sinn Fein members met in Dublin to agree on the formal boycott of Westminster. One week later, they met as, An Dail, i.e. Parliament, in Dublin's Mansion House, and ratified the Irish Republic, declared at Easter 1916. They also selected a cabinet though only 28 members were present; many were in prison. The moral right of the Irish people had been asserted. The new government, under Eamon DeValera, an ex-1916 veteran, would seek international recognition. The Irish people would reject British rule by force of arms, where and when necessary.

Violence against policemen was already occurring. As early as 17 January, the Viceroy, Lord French, had asked Churchill's new Department for extra equipment to fight off Sinn Fein attacks. Winston was only four days in office at that stage and the request was handled by Sir Henry Wilson, who though born in county Longford, was firmly pro-Ulster unionist.

Churchill was advised that the army could only intervene in Ireland, as invited by the Irish authorities, i.e. the Viceroy and Secretary for Ireland. The attacks on police continued. By April, Lord French, who of course knew Winston personally from service in France, wrote directly to him, looking for a huge input of British soldiers, to put down what was becoming an armed rebellion. Churchill reacted cautiously, sending about two thirds of the requested troops. During 1919 a guerilla war continued to develop, with atrocities being committed by both sides. There was an attempt to kill Lord French himself, in the Phoenix Park. The war on the Irish side was coordinated by the Minister for Finance, Michael Collins. Lord French tried to contain the situation by declaring martial law in parts of the country.

PARTITION LOOMS AS WAR CONTINUES

When the situation in Ireland was discussed during the Army Estimates in the Commons in February 1920, Churchill emphasised that his role was purely to assist the civil authorities in Ireland, if requested. He said: "The responsibility of the War Office is limited to providing the necessary troops. The military have had a very difficult task, in Ireland. They have a terrible task. I believe they have far more often erred on the side of weakness, even though it placed them in a foolish position, than on the side of violence...For many years I have been associated with others in this house, seeking to solve the Irish problem, by a measure of self-government. Before the War, the Liberals of those days, extorted from the Irish Nationalist leaders, a definite agreement that Ulster was not to be compelled, against her will, to join a Home Rule Parliament, until two successive General Elections had taken place, which everybody knew was tantamount to saying that she could never join a Dublin Parliament. That is the position the government take up now...If my Right honourable friend (J.G. Devlin Irish Nationalist M.P. for West Belfast) could lead his fellow countrymen to accept the measures now proposed, in the name of all Britain for the first time, and make a genuine effort to work the constitution which will arise from this measure, the day would soon come when this military force, to which he objects and which no doubt is a burden, and whose administration necessarily must be clumsy and galling, would be withdrawn. The day would also come, when after a few years of successful administration by an Irish Parliament on College Green, dealing with the affairs of three parts of Ireland, the fourth part, of her own free will, would come in and associate herself with you".

One month later, the Government brought in a Bill in the Commons for two Parliaments in Ireland, with a Council of Ireland drawn from the two parliaments. The Imperial Parliament would control security, foreign affairs, customs and land. This proposal was rejected by Sinn Fein. The Ulster Unionists had not initially looked for their own Parliament.

They wanted to continue to be ruled directly from Westminster. But when they realised that the British Government wished ultimately to withdraw completely from Ireland, they realised that their own Parliament was essential for their own security.

As Charles Craig said in the Commons on 29 March 1920, "We believe that so long as we were without a Parliament of our own, constant attempts would be made to draw us into a Dublin Parliament. We profoundly distrust the Labour Party and Mr. Asquith". Charles Craig's brother, James, played a crucial part in establishing that the new Northern Parliament would cover only six of the nine counties of Ulster. Within those counties Protestants would have 66% of the population as against 57% in Ulster as a whole. This was deemed a much more secure majority. James Craig had quite a job selling this change to the wider Unionist community as the Ulster Covenant had applied to all nine counties. The Protestants of Cavan, Donegal and Monaghan, as well as those in the rest of Ireland were to be sacrificed, mirroring what would shortly happen to Nationalists within the six counties, as Sinn Fein abandoned them. James Craig, who was a Junior Minister in the Imperial Government, which was in two minds about the matter, had a long interview with Lloyd George just before the decisive Cabinet meeting. Craig convinced him that the security of the Unionists would be best secured within a six county statelet, with a possible boundary commission to fine tune the border.

The war in Ireland continued to deteriorate, with the crown forces becoming more and more involved in reprisals against the civilian community. Many people, including a strong Irish-American lobby, were outraged at this. Yet Churchill's sympathies, not unnaturally, were completely with the military, as he explained in the Commons: "It is not only a very wrong thing, but a very dangerous thing to shoot soldiers who fought in the War, who have come home from the War, expecting to have a period of rest and peace, and who do not expect to be murdered from behind hedgerows in a civilised country, by a population for whose defence, they risked their lives during the War". The killings went on.

CHURCHILL'S BLACK AND TANS

In May Lloyd George wrote to Churchill saying that the situation in Ireland couldn't be left as it was. He said that DeValera, "has practically challenged the British Empire, and unless he is put down, the Empire will look silly". The new military commander in Ireland, General Macready, was proposing a massive reinforcement of the security forces of up to eight extra battalions. A government conference on the matter, chaired by Bonar Law and attended by Churchill, was in agreement with the plan, but was advised that such troop movements might affect national security. Churchill then, proposed another solution, that of raising a force of eight thousand ex-soldiers, who would support the police in Ireland. He was angry that the murders in Ireland were going unpunished. He told the government committee: "What strikes me is the feebleness of the local machinery. After a person is caught, he should pay the penalty within a week. Look at the tribunals which the Russian Government have devised. You should get three or four judges, whose scope would be universal, and they should move quickly over the country and do summary justice. Get three Generals, if you cannot get three judges".

He told Lloyd George that he had agreed a month earlier that there should be hangings, as the latter asked, "can you get convictions from Catholics?". In June Winston wrote in true jingoistic tone"... The ordinary Englishman or Scotsman, does not want to be bothered about Ireland or anything else. He wants to build his house... but he has not forgotten he is a conqueror...he will rouse himself to action. Meanwhile, no course is open to the government but to take every possible measure to break the murder campaign and to enforce the authority of the law, while at the same time, pressing forward the Home Rule Bill". The Cabinet decided to set up a cabinet committee on Ireland with Winston as chairman. Other members were Balfour, Lord Birkenhead (F.E. Smith), and Sir James Craig an Ulster Unionist. Churchill adopted a policy of advocating attacking suspected military groups from the air. He believed that to gain peace, the authorities had to hit the rebels hard. He was advised that the situation on the ground had changed drastically since before the War, with the general population supporting the rebels. Even civil servants could not be trusted. Churchill was adamant that the rule of law must prevail. One of his wilder proposals to cabinet was that a force of 30,000 loyal Ulstermen, be recruited to uphold, 'the authority of the Crown', in all of Ireland. Sir Hammar Greenwood, the Irish Secretary,introduced a measure in the Commons to suspend jury trials and replace them by courts martial. This was to offset the level of intimidation, he said. Lloyd George declared that the Government would never let Ireland leave the United Kingdom. A little later he said a Home Rule type of settlement could be discussed with any responsible body, excluding Sinn Fein.

    The auxiliary force which had been agreed to by cabinet, at Churchill's initiative, was recruited and sent to Ireland. They were known as the ' Black and Tans ' because of their dress, a mixture of Khaki uniform. General Tudor organised them. They began to make their presence felt immediately, as they responded with extreme viciousness to terrorist incidents. Soon they were regarded by the populace as the real terrorists. General Macready deprecated their reprisal policy to Sir Henry Wilson, who spoke to Churchill on the matter. He would not hear of such criticism, regarding them as honourable and gallant officers. Macready himself then contacted Churchill directly on the matter. Churchill, who was about to go on a painting holiday in France at the time, agreed to have General Tudor called to the War Office to see Wilson. Churchill later had to break his holiday in France before resuming it in Italy, to come to London. There Wilson entreated him to control the Black and Tans and condemn reprisal actions. Winston refused, declaring:"... the greatest help in this respect will be given by the Irish population of towns where troops are quartered, if they not only abstain from murdering the soldiers by treacherous means, but also render the assistance, which is easily in their power to give, for the detection of the actual criminals. I do not think that the state of things is going from bad to worse in Ireland... I see no reason why, with patience and firmness, we may not wear the trouble down in the course of a few years... I do not believe that the discipline of the army has deteriorated in any fundamental sense...care must be taken not to discourage the loyalty and zeal of the troops in defending themselves from cowardly and treacherous attacks". He rejected the criticism that General Macready had made on the auxiliary forces. Neither would he heed Wilson's fears of the reprisals being counterproductive. He had the backing of the Prime Minister on this policy.

In October Churchill wrote to his Irish cousin, Sir Shane Leslie, that there would be no talking with the Irish until the murdering ceased;" as long as the murder conspiracy goes on, things will go from bad to worse; the military power of the British government in Ireland will continually increase". Winston made a major public speech in Dundee making the same point.

Meantime the Government was pressing ahead with the Government of Ireland Bill, for two parliaments in Ireland. The northern Unionists had very reluctantly accepted the measure, giving them a parliament over six counties.

THE SQUALID WAR

The Cabinet also discussed the issue of reprisals by the army, but refused to declare them official. But Winston supported an official reprisal policy saying it was not fair on the army which was carrying out the reprisals. He also called for 'each Irish person to have to carry an identity card and a passport for travel to Great Britain'. On 4 November, he said, "The Irish murder gang is a world-wide conspiracy against our country, designed to deprive us of our place in the world and rob us of victory". He was provided with an armed guard as intelligence reports said that Sinn Fein had plans to kidnap a member of the cabinet.

In November the Black and Tans took reprisals in Cork city after four army officers disappeared off a train. In Dublin fourteen alleged British spies were shot by Sinn Fein; among them six army officers. The latter were commemorated by a service at Westminster Abbey, attended by Churchill. On the following day, fifteen Black and Tans were shot dead in county Cork. The cabinet dithered, unwilling to accept Henry Wilson's and General Macready's advice of the need for a major military onslaught. Wilson wanted martial law declared in all of Ireland. Churchill advocated selected areas, for which he would make the necessary troops available. He also advocated putting up rewards for the capture of Sinn Feiners in Great Britain. Finally the cabinet, fearing the handing over of too much control to the military, agreed to impose martial law in part of Munster. The next day which was 13 December, one Black and Tan was shot dead in Cork city. His colleagues ran amok and burned down a large part of the city.

Two days later Winston spoke on the Army Estimates Debate in the Commons: "Ireland bulks very largely in our minds because it is the heart's centre of the British Empire. Any disturbance or movement there, produces vibrations, almost convulsions, throughout almost the whole of the system of society". Churchill claimed that monies for the Black and Tans came from the Irish Office and not the Army Estimates. J.G. Devlin, the northern nationalist M.P. made an impassioned plea to Churchill to call off the Black and Tans, who were," terrorising the people who are guilty of no offence. If the right honourable gentleman had any regard for the honour of the Forces which he controls, let him put an end to these things. You have been preaching peace and you are anxious for peace. Is it upon these grim foundations that the fabric of peace is to be built?".

Churchill replied: "I have a great measure of sympathy with my hon. Friend because he is fighting as well as he can, with all his might and main, for the cause of his country and he is fighting for it by constitutional methods. In my opinion, it takes a great deal more pluck to stand up day after day against a necessarily hostile House of Commons than it does to lie behind a hedge, waiting to shoot some poor Irish constable when he is on his way home to his wife and children after his days work is done... So far as Ireland is concerned, who began this new strife? We did not begin it. Until about 150 policemen and soldiers had been shot dead, there was no disturbance and disorder in Ireland of the kind my hon. Friend has made such great complaint... Let murder stop, let constitutional dominion begin, let the Irish people carry the debate from the squalid conditions in which it is now being pushed forward by the Irish murder gang - (An interrupting M.P. shouts 'And by the Government'). Let them carry this debate into the field of fair discussion. Let them press their constitutional claims, as all the people of the British Isles have a right to do, in the great constitutional Parliamentary assemblies of the Nation, and they will find that instantly there will be a release of all those harsh and lamentable conditions which are bringing misery upon Ireland, and undoubtedly bringing discredit upon the whole of the British Empire".

Herbert Asquith had regained his parliamentary seat in February 1920 to head the Independent Liberal group in Parliament. Despite his record of suppressing the Dublin 1916 Rising with such ferocity, he spoke vehemently against the "hellish policy of reprisals" in Ireland. Asquith tried to lead his group of Liberals out of the wilderness but did not find it easy to make up with Lloyd George. Churchill attacked the Independent Liberals speaking at the 1920 Club: "They tell us how much better men they are than we are, how much more consistent... have stood carefully aside from the burden and heat of the day". Winston was bitter with Asquith for 'deserting him over the Dardanelles' and not appointing him to the Ministry of Munitions in 1916. Churchill's wife was not pleased with how her husband spoke of the old man, Asquith, but he declined to take her advice of 'be a dove and put it right'.

The Catholic Archbishop of Tuam in county Galway, wrote to Churchill telling him that a truce was essential for peace, as the ordinary people were fully behind Sinn Fein. On 29 December Lloyd George, in cabinet, proposed a short term truce. Winston backed him. But this was opposed totally by the security people, who asked for an extension of martial law to other counties. This view prevailed. The Irish Secretary then began to report that the rebels were at "the maximum of which they are capable". He was pleased to report that the Irish Catholic bishops, who condemned government violence, also condemned all "methods of violence" as being against the law of the Church.

JENNIE CHURCHILL'S IRISH SYMPATHIES

Churchill left the immediate area of responsibility for Ireland, when in February, he moved from the War Office to become Secretary of State for the Colonies. His wife knew that this would not remove him from the Irish burden. She wrote him a remarkable letter from which it is obvious that she was very au fait and sympathetic with the Irish issue. She chided him for obduracy, where Ireland was concerned:

"Do my darling use your influence now for some sort of moderation or at any rate justice in Ireland. Put yourself in the place of the Irish. If you were their leader you would not be cowed by severity and certainly not by reprisals, which fall like the rain from Heaven upon the Just and upon the Unjust... It always makes me unhappy and disappointed, when I see you inclined to take for granted that the rough, iron-fisted 'Hunnish' way will prevail".

A BONUS FROM IRELAND

But there was at least some good news for Churchill connected with Ireland in early 1921. He inherited an Irish legacy. His first cousin, Lord Herbert Vane-Tempest, was killed in a train accident in Wales. Lord Herbert had property in Ireland from which he derived a good income. He was a bachelor and left his estate to his cousin. Winston immediately bought a Rolls Royce. He began to investigate properties near London, where he would love to have a country retreat for himself and the family. Chartwell, with eighty acres, was his choice.

FAMILY TRAGEDIES

The rest of 1921 brought many heartaches to Winston and his wife. In March Clementine's brother, Bill, whom Winston had bailed out of gambling debts on several occasions shot himself in a Paris hotel room. In May Jennie Churchill suffered a bad fall and died suddenly in June. Writing to Lord Curzon, Winston said of her: "I do not feel a sense of tragedy, but only of loss...The wine of life was in her veins. Sorrows and storms were conquered by her nature and on the whole it was a life of sunshine". But worse, much worse was to follow in August, when their three year old daughter, Marigold, died with Winston and Clementine at her bedside. His wife's shrieks of agony reminded Winston of an animal in mortal pain.

The Author is shown around Aras an Uachtarain by President Robinson. Winston's Grandfather lived here while Viceroy and Winston stayed here while on his Boer War lecture tour in 1900.

CHAPTER 8

YOU SAW DEVALERA WITHOUT ANY PRECONDITIONS

Winston's new post, the Colonial Office, was responsible for matters affecting the self governing Dominions. Almost immediately within the cabinet, he felt a new freedom to approach Ireland from a different attitude, now that he was not responsible for the army. DeValera had written to Lloyd George suggesting that they should meet for talks. The cabinet turned down this request, believing that DeValera could not control the Sinn Fein gunmen whose allegiance was to Michael Collins. The cabinet then considered whether it should go ahead with the two elections in Ireland, for the two new parliaments. Winston was firmly in favour of holding them saying, "The elections would be a new situation which might lead to negotiations". This view prevailed. The cabinet then had to consider whether a truce should be called. The Times had published a letter from the bishops of England on 6 April condemning the practice of indiscriminate and unauthorised reprisals by the irregular forces of the crown and urging a truce. Churchill spoke forcefully in favour of a truce at cabinet on 12 May:

"I am one of the few who holds the same opinion today and yesterday. It is of great public importance to get a respite in Ireland. I don't agree that it would be a sign of weakness. It would be six or eight months ago. Then we were not in a position to make any concessions and we had to stand firm and we did so. Now our forces are stronger and better trained; auxiliaries are stronger; the police are extending their control over the country; our position is vastly better in a material sense; our position is not better from point of view of reaching finality; no great difficulty in going on for a year or two; very unpleasant as regards this country all over the world; we are getting an odious reputation; poisoning our relations with the United States; it is in our power to go on and enlist constables and Black and Tans; but we should do everything to get a way to a settlement...

If you are strong enough you should make the effort. Where is the disadvantage? There is no military disadvantage. Supposing you appeal to Irish honour. If you do attempt to appease, either the truce will be kept or it will be broken. If kept you'll have tremendous advantage; They'll have great difficulty in getting men to go back; if they break you are in a far stronger position with our public opinion; your troops are all in position; they can begin at any moment and in the interval you'll have got information. It is a matter of psychology when you should time it, but it should be very early and allow a gentler mood to prevail".

Despite Churchill's views, the cabinet feared a truce might enable Sinn Fein to regroup and restock arms. It came out against a truce. The two elections took place on 24 May.

NORTHERN PARLIAMENT OPENED BY KING

In the North, the Unionists won forty seats with Sinn Fein and the Nationalists winning twelve. James Craig, who had been chosen ahead of Carson as the leader of the Ulster Unionists, abandoned Westminister, and returned to Ulster to become

Prime Minister. The Government of Ireland Act came into effect formally when on 23 June 1921 the King opened the new Parliament of Northern Ireland. The King, with government approval, made a sincere speech appealing to all Irish people to join in, "a new era of peace, contentment and goodwill". Churchill was very impressed by the King's words and wrote congratulating him on a visit which, "I am sure will help materially to facilitate the reunion of the two islands". In the south Sinn Fein were victorious but refused to attend a Southern Parliament which would only rule a part of the island. The only attenders at this parliament were the four Unionists from Trinity College. It never met again.

Negotiations carried on within Ireland and with Britain on a possible truce. The King's speech created a climate and an urgency for a peace conference. DeValera consulted the southern Unionists who emphasised to the British the need for peace. The government sent General Smuts, the South African leader to Dublin to talk to DeValera to find out what were the parameters within which they might settle. He reported to ministers that Sinn Fein believed they could attain a Republic. Smuts had floated the idea of a Dominion status, which had not been rejected out of hand.

CHURCHILL SUPPORTS TRUCE

Eventually DeValera wrote to Lloyd George saying he was, 'ready to meet and discuss, the basis upon which the proposed conference can reasonably hope to achieve the desired object'. With Churchill's strong support Lloyd George decided to call a truce. The Irish Times reported: "The following press notice was issued last night in London: 'In accordance with the Prime Minister's offer and Mr. DeValera's reply, arrangements are being made for the hostilities to cease from Monday next 11 July, at noon'". Sir Henry Wilson's view of the matter was; "So the murderers have won and the coward Lloyd George has gone down on his knees and all his miserable cabinet on their hunkers behind him".

DeValera arrived at ten Downing St. on 14 July to see Lloyd George, while outside a huge crowd of Irish people welcomed him. Lloyd George was unsure how much power DeValera really had. DeValera emphasised that he felt that the six county northern state might be the main difficulty. Lloyd George was seeing James Craig in London at the same time. Craig told him: "In no circumstances "would Northern Ireland join a Dublin Parliament where its representation would be in proportion to its population. Lloyd George warned DeValera that his position on the north might lead to a civil war. He replied that the South would rather "let the north alone" than be implicated in a civil war. On 20 July Lloyd George gave DeValera his government's proposals allowing the South, Dominion Status, which included power over the army, police and financial matters. In practice this offer was quite considerably more, than what had been offered in the Government of Ireland Act 1920. But the British stood firm on the high ground of constitutional principle. As in 1921 British monarchical and Irish republican symbols were irreconcilable. For both leaders it was the symbols of sovereignty that signified most. General Jan Smuts had writen to DeValera in June: "I have been through the same troubles in my own country. The best years of my life were spent in the same struggle through which you have been passing...start as a full Dominion in the South, and it will not be long before the North will agree to join hands with you freely and willingly". Three weeks later, DeValera rejected the offer demanding 'complete independence in Southern

Ireland', unless the North joined the Irish Dominion. An impasse developed and DeValera returned to Dublin. He asked Lloyd George not to publish the proposals but that he, DeValera, would send on counter proposals.

The British cabinet rejected DeValera's claim to independence. In September the King expressed a view that his government should not issue any ultimatum. DeValera wrote to Lloyd George who felt that an organised conference with a time frame, was needed to thrash out an agreement. There was disagreement within cabinet as to whether it should lay down preconditions for such a conference. Churchill thought not, though he was ready for a resumption of hostilities, should the talks prove futile. He said:

"It is too late in the controversy to invite these people to an unconditional conference. In the first instance you saw DeValera without any preconditions. To allow them to come unconditionally would be to admit tacitly that the British empire is an open question. We are at the end of our thether but they are not at the end of theirs. They have a great fear in their hearts. I believe you will help them to reason if your reply brings them right up against it. I propose a direct question to them - 'If you wish to come to a conference on the basis of the integrity of the Empire, come, if not, not.' The cabinet should not assume it is going to be a terrible war and I am fortified in my view by the language used by General Macready. It will not be much worse than what has gone on before. We have taken the ground which the world approves. My view was that coercion should be on fundamentals, not on finance...".

The Cabinet decided to invite DeValera to a conference to explore 'how the association of Ireland with the community of nations, known as the British Empire, can best be reconciled with Irish national aspirations'. It set up a Committee of nine

Ministers, "with full powers to deal with the Irish situation which would arise out of the reply which was being sent to DeValera that day". Winston was a committee member.

WINSTON SETS PARAMETERS

Churchill decided to publicise his views on the forthcoming conference by making a major speech in his Dundee constituency on 24 September setting down the limits to which he would agree to:

"How could they agree to the setting up of a separate foreign Republic in Ireland? How could anyone suppose that peace could be found along that road? Not peace, but certain war - real war, not mere bushranging, would follow from such a course. Great Britain would always live in apprehension, which he dared say would be well founded, that Ireland was intriguing against us with other foreign countries, giving submarine bases, or providing facilities for strangling our life and trade. The only effective check which they could have upon such activities, apart from going to war, would be to erect a tariff wall between Great Britain and Ireland...

If war broke out between the British Empire and the Irish Republic - and in his opinion it certainly would - every Irishman in the British Empire would become an alien enemy, and would be in exactly the same position as the unfortunate Germans who were in this country during the Great War. What a hideous and idiotic prospect unfolded to their eyes! What a crime they would commit if, seeking a brief interval from war, they condemned themselves and their children to such misfortunes. They should be ripping the British Empire and preparing certain war at no distant date - a war in which Britain would be called to the aid of Ulster, and in which the new Republic would do their best to embroil their kith and kin in the United States. They could not do this !...Squander this conference and peace is bankrupt".

Even the Times, no friend of Winston's, felt compelled to write :" The country should be grateful to Mr. Churchill for the breadth and lucidity of his speech... whether men agree with him or not, Mr. Churchill's able and calm review of the situation helps to restore confidence".

The Irish demanded that several of their imprisoned leaders, including Arthur Griffith, should be released. This was agreed to because it could make the difference," between success and failure of negotiations". Churchill went along with this move. The Cabinet also spent a lot of time deciding on policy should the Conference fail. They warned particularly that there should be no sudden end to it, which might put British troops in Ireland at a disadvantage. Arthur Balfour and Austen Chamberlain were the Ministers most doubtful about appeasing DeValera. Churchill believed all along that the British would easily pacify Ireland, if it wished to launch an all out offensive. But this was to be a resort of final measure, in his view. The British were perplexed by not knowing clearly who was the real Irish leader. Titularly it was DeValera, but they strongly suspected that the de facto leader was Michael Collins. It was he they feared most. DeValera had been away from Ireland in the United States during most of the war and it was Collins who had led the fight against the British. When DeValera returned, there was a certain amount of rivalry between himself and Collins. The latter was most suspicious of the coming Conference. He was afraid that his war machine too might be put at a disadvantage during any truce period.

Despite all the misgivings agreement was reached by both sides to attend a Conference at ten Downing St. on 11 October. The Irish Parliament (Dail) choose its delegation on 9

The first Irish delegation to London, July 12 1921: R. C. Barton, Eamon de Valera, Count George Plunkett, Arthur Griffith and Erskine Childers.

September. To everyone's surprise it did not contain DeValera. This decision gave rise to more suspicion as Collins, who was on the delegation, feared he was being set up by DeValera, who realised from his July meetings with Lloyd George, that an Irish Republic was unattainable. The British were not sorry DeValera was not coming as Lloyd George had found him almost impossible to deal with during the summer. DeValera explained his controversial decision which was against the will of the majority of the other members of the cabinet in a letter to the Irish-American leader, Joseph McGarrity:

"1. To avoid compromising the Republic, of which being head I was a symbol...

2. I wished to remain here as a reserve against tricks of Lloyd George...

3. If the proposal of External Association were to be accepted by the British, I would need all the influence I could command here to get those republicans who desire isolation to consent...

Having decided that I should remain at home, it was necessary that Collins and Griffith should go. That Griffith would accept the Crown under pressure, I had no doubt. From the preliminary work which Collins was doing with the I.R.B. (Irish Republican Brotherhood), of which I had heard something, and from my own weighing up of him, I felt certain that he too was contemplating accepting the Crown, but I had hoped that all this would simply make them both a better bait for Lloyd George, leading him on and on, further in our direction. I felt convinced on the other hand that as matters came to a close we would be able to hold them from this side from crossing the line".

ONLY LLOYD GEORGE SHAKES HANDS

The formidable secretary to the Irish Delegation was an Englishman who had served with the British army in the Boer and Great Wars, Erskine Childers. He was a recent convert to Irish republicanism and a zealot in the cause. The British choose their delegation on 6 October. It consisted of Lloyd George, Lord Birkenhead, Worthington-Evans, Hammar Greenwood, Austen Chamberlain, the Attorney-General and Winston Churchill. Both sides met across the table in the conference room at ten Downing St on 11 October. There were three fundamental issues before them: the future constitutional status of Ireland; whether the island was to be reunited or remain partitioned; and British security and defence requirements. The Prime Minister was the only British delegate to shake hands with the Irish delegation. Lloyd George opened the Conference by referring to the great opportunity they had to solve the differences between the two countries.

A 'Committee on the Observance of the Truce' was set up very early on, to thrash out details about what could and could not be allowed to occur on the military front, during the peace. The British were annoyed that the Sinn Fein army, called the Irish Republican Army (I.R.A.), continued to drill openly. The opening of Sinn Fein Courts was particularly embarrassing too. The importation of arms was to be disallowed. A shipment of arms had been discovered in Hamburg en route to the I.R.A. When the discovery was brought to Collins' attention in London, he dispatched one of his bodyguards to Germany to ensure the safety of the cargo. The person so instructed was the young son of the executed Major John MacBride, of the Irish Brigade in the Boer War and the Dublin 1916 Rising, Sean MacBride. The movement of troops by either side had to be notified. Three days notice of a resumption of hostilities was agreed to. A White Paper on "Arrangements Governing the Cessation of Active operations in Ireland" was published on 26 October.

POLITICAL DANGERS FOR GOVERNMENT

Lloyd George and Winston Churchill realised very clearly that the effort to pacify Ireland was a highly dangerous political move, as their Tory coalition partners were very doubtful about it. The Tories were due to meet in Party conference in Liverpool that November, where it was expected a critical response would be made to the negotiations. The formal agreement reached on the Truce meant little in practice as on the ground both sides prepared for a resumption of hostilities.

Churchill was made Chairman of another Committee to consider air and naval defence matters. He was advised by the Navy that it felt control of Irish ports was of little importance.

But Lloyd George was insisting that Britain retained control over some, which they could return later if they so wished. Winston's position then became:

'We must have free use of the Irish coasts in peace or war for Imperial defence '. Bear Island, Queenstown: Lough Swilly, which is used for manoeuvres and important for guarding the commerce of Liverpool, that we can arrange with the Dominion of Northern Ireland'. The Irish rejected this and produced their own paper calling for Irish control over all ports. Churchill retorted:

"This able memorandum will shorten the task of this committee, in fact will bring it to an end. It amounts to a reasoned, measured, uncompromising refusal to meet us at any point. It advances the theory to which we could not become a party - that Ireland is a foreign Ireland...The right to build an Irish navy is claimed. I regard this as a mortal blow." At a later date Churchill gave vent to his feelings of political vulnerability, which the Irish did not appear to fully comprehend when he said: "We are taking great political risks. The life of the Government is put in issue by our proposals. We were prepared to face that because it is worthwhile taking risks to get a reconciliation between your great race and ours. To end the feud is worth the risk of our political life, but these incidents will make it impossible. We must know your attitude on certain vital questions. Is allegiance to the King to be finally repudiated? Can you under no condition accept the sovereignty of the King in the sense that India and Australia accept it? Is the communicating link of the Crown to be snapped forever? Are you prepared to be associated with the fraternity of Nations known as the British Empire? Do you accept in principle that we must take necessary measures to give us facilities for our security not as a treaty which can be cancelled, but as a fundamental part of an arrangement ?".

WINSTON REJECTS IRISH NEUTRALITY

Churchill saw the Sinn Fein memorandum as a claim to neutrality. His problem with that was: "we cannot be sure that the Irish would have power to keep an effective neutrality. We could not guarantee the confluence of trade in an area where submarines were lurking unless we had Queenstown and other ports". Michael Collins interrupted Churchill at that point to ask :" Mr. Churchill, do not you agree that if neutrality were a greater safeguard to you than anything else, it would be a greater value to you than your proposals?". To which Winston replied :" I do not accept that. A completely honest neutrality by Ireland in the last war would have been far worse for us. Ireland's control of her neutrality might be ineffective".

Michael Collins wrote to 'President DeValera' on 12 October from the 'Irish Delegation of Plenipotentiaries' in which he said that Erskine Childers would have briefed DeValera about things yesterday - "I have never felt so relieved at the end of any day, and I need hardly say I am not looking forward with any pleasure to resumption - such a crowd I never met... Good luck. This place bloody limit. I wish to God I were back home".

Another major point of dissention was whether Ireland would accept allegiance to the Crown. It emerged that they would not do so, if Ireland was to be divided into two States. Griffith said that as long as the British backed up the Ulster Unionists, the latter will not yield up one inch. He claimed that neither Fermanagh nor Tyrone should have been included into the northern statelet. He also believed that if a county by county vote had been held, Derry and Armagh would have voted against partition.

The Irish offered to give Ulster all her 'existing powers and possibly more' if 'she accepted the position of a provincial legislature and came into the central Dublin Parliament'. This offer put the British side in a dilemma. They saw the logic of the proposal and they did not want to let Ulster ruin the chances of a settlement. Churchill saw the merits of the proposal, but he felt trapped. He said:

"We can't give way on the six counties; we are not free agents; we can do our best to include the Six in a larger Parliament plus autonomy. We could press Ulster to hold autonomy for Six from them instead of from us". Lord Birkenhead, Winston's best friend, agreed, saying: "I rather agree with Winston; our position re Six counties is an impossible one if these men want to settle, as they do". Churchill added: "I don't see how Ulster is damnified: she gets her own protection, an effective share in the Southern Parliament and protection for the Southern Unionists".

Another committee was then established to 'explore the Ulster question'. It transpired that Partition was the main stumbling block for the Irish. They were willing to solve the matter of allegiance to the Crown and the Empire, if a form of unity could be reached. Lloyd George said that he would be willing to consider 'any machinery by which the unity of Ireland could be organised or strengthened'.

CHAPTER 9

NEGOTIATING WITH THE REBELS

The formal part of the Conference finished at the end of October. But crucial informal sessions and private meetings continued to occur. Churchill was to the fore in organising such get togethers over dinner tables, where he was so used to conducting successful business. He seemed to come to be on particularly good terms with Michael Collins. "Churchill was fascinated by Collins, and the compliment was returned". Although early in the Conference Collins was very wary of Winston writing of him: "will sacrifice all for political gain... studies, I imagine, the detail carefully - thinks about his constituents, effects of so and so on them. Inclined to be bombastic. Full of ex-officer jingo or similar outlook. Don't actually trust him".

On Sunday night of 30 October, Winston invited Lloyd George and Birkenhead along with Collins and Griffith to dine with him at his home in Sussex Gardens. It was essential to have Birkenhead because 'he would control most of the Unionists'. On Thomas Jones' (Secretary to the British Delegation) advice, Lloyd George saw Griffith alone for most of the evening, as Jones understood that the two Irish distrusted Churchill and Birkenhead. Lloyd George advised Griffith that he would be able to carry a six county parliament subordinate to the national parliament in Dublin. He also mentioned the idea of a Boundary Commission, which might make changes to the existing border. Meantime the other three gentlemen sought to indulge in social banter. Churchill wrote that Collins was in a very difficult mood that evening, reproachful and defiant, complaining how the British 'hunted me night and day' adding, 'you put a price on my head'. At that Winston produced a proclamation the Boers had issued about himself in 1899, offering £25 for his head. When Collins saw the poster, he laughed heartily and he became less irritable. After that meeting Collins believed that a 'united Ireland' recognising the Crown and safeguarding the Ulster Unionists and remaining as part of the Commonwealth was possible. Lloyd George spoke in Parliament the next day where he was very pleased that the vote on the Irish matter was carried by 439 votes to 43. But when he saw James Craig and the Ulster Unionists, he despaired of getting any cooperation from them which would help. He believed that if Craig would cede Fermanagh and Tyrone to the South, agreement would be reached. Lloyd said that he would consider resigning and force a General Election if a settlement could not be achieved on these plans. He was prepared to resume the war with the southern Irish, if they didn't accept the essentials. But he would equally fight the Tory-Unionists if they did not accept minimum concessions. Lloyd George was particularly suspicious of Bonar Law who was an outright Orangeman. He feared that he might be the one to lead a Tory revolt from within the Government and use it as a pretext to try to become Prime Minister. Lloyd George met James Craig on 7 November, but again got nowhere. George considered resignation. He believed that Birkenhead and Chamberlain might go with him, but he was unsure of Churchill. The Prime Minister did not want to coerce the South. The only possible alternative was that if the South would settle for a twenty six county Dominion, with the promise of a boundary commission. Griffith and Collins refused to countenance this as it 'sacrificed unity'. If he resigned, Lloyd George expected Bonar Law to succeed him.

Talk of resignation roused Churchill and he warned the P.M. of the consequences in a letter on 9 November: "The criticism will certainly be made that the government in resigning have abdicated their responsibility. More especially will this charge be made if the reason given is 'we are debarred by honour from coercing the North, and by conviction from coercing the south'. It will be said, 'here are men united in principle, knowing what they ought to do and what the interests require, who are possessed of an overwhelming Parliamentary majority, including a majority of their own followers, who nevertheless without facing Parliament, throw down the commission and declare themselves incapable of action in any direction.

I greatly fear the consequences of such tactics, no matter how lofty may be the motives which prompt them.

After this has occurred, Mr. Bonar Law will be invited to form a government. Why should he not do so? Surely he would be bound in honour to do so, if the members of the present Government have declared themselves to be inhibited from moving in any direction. Why should he not succeed ?... In the crisis under consideration, the Conservative Party will have to rally to someone. Obviously they will rally to a conservative leader, forming a Conservative Government, which has come forward to fill the gap created by the suicide of the coalition; and which will be entitled to carry the standard forward against Labour at an imminent election, and to receive considerate treatment from ex-Ministers who have just thrown up the sponge. The delusion that an alternative Government cannot be formed is perennial. Mr. Chamberlain thought Sir Henry Campbell-Bannerman would be 'hissed of the stage'. Mr. Asquith was confident that you could not form an administration. But in neither case did the outgoing administration tie its hands in every direction by proclaiming itself honourably bound to do what the situation might require".

Lloyd George did not resign but resumed negotiations, trying to pressurise Craig into a compromise. The latter refused despite being threatened by a boundary commission, which all the Government (including Tories) agreed would take territory off the North and stultify it economically. Churchill agreed that Southern Ireland should get 'the status of an Irish State, with an All Ireland Parliament, a position in the Imperial Conference and the League of Nation'. The Irish delegation and the Irish Cabinet were split on a draft treaty, particularly over the Oath of Allegiance to the Crown. Collins and Griffith believed that the British would not bend further and that they should sign and put it to the Dail and the people. The delegation, which had returned to Dublin for consultations, were instructed to return to London to tell Lloyd George that the Treaty could not be signed, unless the Oath of allegiance was amended. They were also told that it was now 'a matter for the Dail and to try and put the blame on Ulster'. Even at this late stage DeValera refused entreaties to join the delegation.

Once again the expectation in London was that there would be a breakdown in the talks with war the outcome. Collins and Griffith urged Lloyd George that Craig should recognise 'unity, if the south accepts the Commonwealth' and that they could then sell the agreement to the Dail. Churchill too had been busy looking for formulae to ease the problems. He consulted Harold Laski, a political philosopher and historian who wrote of their encounter:"

...he told me that things were likely to break down upon the problem of allegiance. So I talked at length upon this as a quantitative problem which need not be met in the formal way of the past. The real thing was to get the safeguards of function which came not from an oath exacted, but a conscience satisfied. He seemed impressed, and when I was going asked me to drop in the next day. When I arrived he had the Attorney General with him and asked me to repeat my argument. This I did with amplification, and for one and a half hours we argued up and down. Finally the A-G asked me could I put my views (with which he disagreed) into a formula. I suggested an oath 'to the Irish State and the King in Parliament as the head of the British Commonwealth'. Churchill was very surprised and said it was a new approach. Then explore it, I said: but the A-G was very hostile and I left with a sense of hopelessness. On the Saturday I went to town and had a hurried summons from Winston who said that Lloyd George liked my formula and could I develop the point on paper. This I did, and got a note on Sunday saying that L.G. would put an almost identical formula before the Cabinet on Monday. The Irish were stiff about it but in the end accepted it in return for a full free trade agreement".

BRITISH ULTIMATUM

The Conference resumed formally that same Monday 5 December at three P.M. Lloyd George issued an ultimatum to the Irish that they must sign the draft treaty, as it stood, or accept the consequences of immediate and terrible war. For his own political reasons he had decided against waiting any longer to try to force the Ulster Unionists to compromise. He said: "I have to communicate with Sir James Craig tonight. Here are the alternative letters which I have prepared, one enclosing Articles of Agreement reached by His Majesty's Government and yourselves and the other stating that the Sinn

Fein representatives refuse to come within the Empire. If I send this letter it is war, and war within three days. Which letter am I to send ?". He realised that to try to coerce Ulster would lead to the collapse of his government and Bonar Law becoming P.M. His own political future was on the line. Arthur Griffith had earlier given him assurances that if Ulster refused to agree to an All Ireland Parliament then it could vote to remain at Westminster. The dramatic scene at ten Downing St. has been captured by Churchill himself:

"The Prime Minister stated bluntly that we could concede no more and debate no further. They must settle now; they must sign the agreement for a Treaty in the form to which after all these weeks it had attained, or else quit; and further, that both sides would be free to resume whatever warfare they could wage against each other. This was an ultimatum delivered, not through diplomatic channels, but face to face, and all present knew and understood that nothing else was possible. Stiff as our personal relations had been, there was by now a mutual respect between the principals and a very deep comprehension of each other's difficulties.

The Irishmen gulped down the ultimatum phlegmatically. Mr. Griffith said, speaking in his soft voice and with his modest manner, 'I will give the answer of the Irish delegates at nine tonight; but, Mr. Prime Minister, I personally will sign this agreement and will recommend it to my countrymen'. 'Do I understand, Mr. Griffith,' said Lloyd George, 'that though everyone else refuses you will nevertheless agree to sign?'

'Yes, that is so Mr. Prime Minister,' replied this quiet little man of great heart and of great purpose. Michael Collins rose looking as if he was going to shoot someone, preferably himself. In all my life I have never seen so much passion and suffering in restraint".

A DESPERATE DILEMMA

The Irish delegation returned to their quarters. It was a desperate dilemma. The terms on offer represented a remarkable achievement, considering the failure of the much more modest Home Rule plan less than a decade earlier. On the other hand the deal was far short of the independent Republic that so many people in the independence movement had set their sights on. It was no surprise that Griffith would sign; he knew the path that had been trod and was happy to accept the offer. But the announcement by Collins that he too would sign, shook the rest of the delegation. Collins was the epitome of the flamboyant gunman who had carried the fight to the British and forced them to the negotiating table. The other negotiators - Barton, Gavan Duffy and Duggan - were overshadowed by comparison with Griffith and Collins, but they were nonetheless impressive figures. Barton was a Protestant who as a British army officer, had helped suppress the 1916 Dublin Rising. He was a cousin of Erskine Childers. Both Duggan and Gavan-Duffy were lawyers. The debate on signing raged for two hours. Duggan was converted but the other two held out.

Erskine Childers kept a diary of the evenings events:

"They (i.e. the British) directly threatened war. Meeting lasted four hours (to) 7.P.M. (I sat outside reading Lincoln). Home to dinner.

Redraft came. Meeting of delegates at 9 p.m. Final discussion. A.G. (Arthur Griffith) spoke almost passionately for signing. It seems other side insisted all delegates shall sign and recommend treaty to Dail. Monstrous demand. M.C. (Michael Collins) said nothing. Bob Barton refused to sign and G.D. (Gavan Duffy): then long and hot argument, all about war and committing our young men to die, die for nothing: what would G.D. get better? etc., etc. G.D. then assented quietly, Bob shaken. Asked me out and I said it was Principle and I felt Molly (Childer's wife) was with us. Suddenly he said 'well I suppose I must sign'... He went in and said he would sign under duress and solely because if he didn't the country would get no opportunity to decide.

Earlier in the evening at seven o'clock the British delegation assembled in Chamberlain's room in the Commons. Jones, who was present, wrote that Churchill was adamant that unless the Irish replied by ten, they should be assured, 'as to what we are going to do'. The ten o'clock deadline passed and the British began to believe that they would not see the Irish again. Suddenly it was announced that the Irish were on their way. Negotiations resumed again at 11.15 p.m. Childers' Diary resumes: "I outside all time 11.15-2.45 a.m. Saw nothing. Home at 3 a.m. My chief recollection of these inexpressibly miserable hours was that of Churchill in evening dress moving up and down the lobby with his loping stoop and long strides and a huge cigar like a bowsprit. His coarse heavy jowls making him a very type of brutal (word missing). Duggan left by 8.30 a.m. mail for Dublin with the signed Treaty. A.G. said we were on top of the wave. Never such terms again".

Churchill's own account of the final hours are :

"The British Representatives were in their places at nine, but it was not until long after midnight that the Irish Delegation appeared. As before, they were superficially calm and very quiet. There was a long pause, or there seemed to be. Then Mr. Griffith said, 'Mr. Prime Minister, the Delegation is willing to sign the agreements, but there are a few points of drafting which perhaps it would be convenient if I mentioned at once.' Thus, by the easiest of gestures, he carried the whole matter into the realm of minor detail, and everyone concentrated upon these points with overstrained interest so as to drive the main issue into the background for ever.

Soon we were talking about the technicalities and verbal corrections, and holding firmly to all these lest worse should befall. But underneath this protective chatter a profound change had taken place in the spirit and atmosphere. We had become allies and associates in a common cause - the cause of the Irish Treaty and of peace between two races and two islands. It was nearly three o'clock in the morning before we separated. But the agreement was signed by all. As the Irishmen rose to leave, the British Ministers upon a strong impulse walked round and for the first time shook hands".

In Dublin the cabinet split on the Treaty just signed with DeValera voting against it. Childers ' Diary says" Went in (to Cabinet) and found Dev head in hands reproaching M.C. with having signed". But a majority of the cabinet supported it and recommended it to the Dail, where it would be debated in bitter and divisive fashion.

CHURCHILL SELLS TREATY IN COMMONS

In London, Churchill had the task of putting the Treaty before the Commons, which he did with a remarkable speech. He set the context by reminding members of the 'grim, grave, and in many cases, shocking realities' of the previous two years in Ireland. He insisted that though Sinn Fein sought 'an independent sovereign republic for the whole of Ireland, including Ulster' his side had demanded 'allegiance to the Crown, membership of the empire, facilities and securities for the Navy and a complete option for Ulster. On Ulster he said:

"It is no longer open to anyone to say that Ulster is barring the way to the rest of Ireland, that Ulster is forbidding the rest of Ireland to have a Government. That is all past. These great sacrifices of opinion have been made by that small but resolute community at a time of great, distressing, and protracted anxiety to them, and they have been made for the sake of their common interests in the British empire. Ulster has boldly said to the rest of Ireland: 'Have the government you choose; we will do our best to make things go right, and as long as you stay within the British Empire, we close no doors in the future.' That, it seems to me, is what Ulster has said, and I repeat that our debt to her is great.'

Churchill expected that Ulster would unite with the South. That is our policy' he said, 'but in her own time'. He then spoke to those people in the Commons and the Dail, who rejected the Treaty.

"I cannot believe that you will find any responsible body of men here or in Ireland, Liberal or Conservative, North or South, soldier or civilian, who would solemnly declare that on the margin of difference remaining between these extreme views and the Treaty, it would be justifiable to lay the land of Ireland waste to the scourge of war, or to drag the name of Great Britain through the dirt in every part of the world. For you cannot embark on such a struggle without being prepared to face conditions of public opinion all over the world, which undoubtedly would be profoundly detrimental to your interests. You could not do it without being prepared to inflict the most fearful injury on the land and people of Ireland.

When we have this Treaty, defective, admittedly, from your point of view, but still a great instrument, I ask: Are the differences between the Treaty and the extreme desire worth the re-embarking on the war? You cannot do it. If you tried, you would not get the people to support you. On the contrary, you would complain in both countries of their leaders, and they would complain with violence and indignation that they were dragged from their hearths to maltreat each other on pretexts which had been reduced to such manageable dimensions.

It is high time that the main body of Irish and British opinion asserted its determination to put a stop to these fanatical quarrels'.

The previous day in the House of Lords, Lord Carson, condemned Lord Curzon for signing the Treaty, Churchill said. In the Dail, he went on, DeValera condemned Michael Collins for the same thing. He added:

"Are we not getting a little tired of all this? These absolutely sincere, consistent, unswerving gentlemen, faithful in all circumstances to their implacable quarrels, seek to mount their respective war horses, in person or by proxy, and to drive at full tilt at one another, shattering and splintering down the lists, to the indescribable misery of the common people and to the utter confusion of our Imperial affairs ?...If we had shown ourselves a feeble nation fat and supine, sunk in sloth, our mission exhausted, our strength gone, our energies abated, our credentials impaired, if we had shown this lack of quality in the struggle from which we have emerged, then indeed there would be some explanation and justification for such misgivings in the breasts of many gathered here.

But when we have just come out of a world war with our record such as it is, in which our armies have broken the German line, in which our navies have carried on the whole sea business of the Allies, in which our finances have sustained Europe, when we have come out of all these dangers, and have shown that we are capable of taking a leading part, if not the leading part, in the great struggle which has overthrown the largest and most powerful military Empires of which there is a record - when all these facts are considered, surely we can afford to carry on these Irish negotiations according to a clear, cool judgement of what is best in the country's interest, without being deflected or deterred from any particular course of action by a wholly unjustifiable self-accusation of humiliation."

THE POWER OF IRELAND

Churchill then spoke of the role of the Irish in British politics and the role of the Irish nation abroad and how important it was for the two countries to be at peace:

"It is a curious reflection to inquire why Ireland should bulk so largely in our lives? How is it that the great English parties are shaken to their foundations, and even shattered, almost every generation, by contact with Irish affairs? Whence did Ireland derive its power to drive Mr. Pitt from office, to drag down Mr. Gladstone in the summit of his career and to draw us who sit here almost to the verge of civil war, from which we were only rescued by the outbreak of the Great War.

Whence does this mysterious power of Ireland come? It is a small, poor, sparsely populated island, lapped about by British sea power, accessible on every side, without iron or coal. How is it that she sways our councils, shakes our parties, and infects us with great bitterness, convulses our passions, and deranges our action? How is it she has forced generation after generation to stop the whole traffic of the British Empire in order to debate her domestic Affairs?

Ireland is not a daughter State. She is a parent nation. The Irish are an ancient race. 'We are too,' said their plenipotentiaries, 'a far-flung nation.' They are intermingled with the whole life of the Empire, and have interests in every part of the Empire wherever the English language is spoken, especially in these new countries with whom we have to look forward to the greatest friendship and countenance, and where the Irish canker has been at work. How often have we suffered in all these generations from this continued hostility?

If we can free ourselves from it, if we can to some extent reconcile the spirit of the Irish nation to the British Empire in the same way as Scotland and Wales have been reconciled, then indeed we shall have secured advantages which may well repay the trouble and uncertainties of the present time". Such was the impact of Winston's speech that only about sixty Tories voted against the Anglo-Irish Treaty in the Commons. But thereafter this group formed the nucleus of a potential Conservative revolt against Lloyd George's leadership of the Coalition. At this time the P.M. bowed out of centre stage in Irish affairs, leaving Winston in charge of liaison with the expected Provisional Government in Dublin. The latter intended that Britain would disengage as quickly as possible. He hoped that the Irish would assume power as early as 1 January 1922, facilitating the withdrawal of troops and auxiliaries. He became Chairman of the cabinet committee on Ireland which met regularly throughout December. He remained optimistic that the transfer of power would take place expeditiously and safely. Some of his biographers regard him as the founder of the modern Irish State.

TO BRING THE PROVISIONAL GOVERNMENT INTO BEING

While on holiday in the south of France in early January, he wrote to the Prince of Wales in praise of the Irish:

"The Irish event seems to turn well. Arthur Griffith and Michael Collins are men of their word. It was said, 'Irishmen have every form of courage except moral courage'. But one cannot say that any more. When the Treaty was signed after a dramatic struggle, we shook hands on it and pledged ourselves to put it through on both sides without regard to personal or political fortunes. They are certainly doing their part; and we will not fail in ours.

The P.M. has handed the business over to me now: and I am to hurry back from this delightful villa (Lady Essex's) where I have had a few sunny days, to bring the Irish Provisional Government into being at the earliest moment. In spite of all that may be said on the other side - terrible and unanswerable things - I am full of hope and confidence about Ireland. I believe we are going to reap a rich reward all over the world and at home".

The British envisaged that the establishment of autonomy would pass through three stages - the setting up of a temporary Provisional Government upon the approval of the Treaty,the clothing of that body with legal powers upon the passing of legislation, and the emergence of the Government of the Irish Free State when the Constitution had been formally enacted. The Irish administration established on 14 January 1922, had in Churchill's view no separate existence in law. It was merely a suitable arrangement.

A TERRIBLY INCONSIDERATE MAN

Winston's wife joined her husband in France after the Christmas. She was still not well after the trauma of the death of Marigold. During her brief time in France with Winston she again became pregnant. This restored her spirits and good health. Winston's secretary has said that the couple never shared a bedroom. He only shared her room when he got a written invitation. It was explained to the secretary that Clementine liked to go to bed early, while he usually stayed up very late reading or writing. The same secretary said he was the most unselfconscious person she ever met. He would explain that when he had an idea in his mind he became simply unaware of what was going on around him. The secretary said that she was no more to him than a fountain pen that required no time to eat or rest.. "he was a terribly inconsiderate man. In fact I have never known anyone who was so inconsiderate. It wasn't that he was cruel, but he was so involved in his own wishes, his own desires to get the work done that he never thought about the person who had to do it. He always rushed to Clementine with any new idea. She would tell him what she thought of it and there might be a heated argument. He called her his pussycat because 'she spits at me'. They constantly wrote letters or notes to each other, even within Chartwell.

CHAPTER 10

DEALING WITH COLLINS AND CRAIG

The Anglo-Irish Treaty split all sections of the Irish people. To many it was far short of the Republic which had been the aim. But for others, including Michael Collins, it was a start, something tangible, something which would remove the British presence from most of the country after several hundreds of years. The Dail approved the Treaty by the small majority of seven votes, sixty four to fifty seven. President DeValera resigned in protest. Arthur Griffith was then elected President. Throughout the country the I.R.A. split on the issue too. Each side decided to dig in and hold the control it had in the countryside and towns. Those who accepted the Treaty were regarded as traitors by its opponents. Even families were split.

In London Winston Churchill, whose ministerial portfolio covered both parts of Ireland, foresaw difficulties. On the day the Treaty was narrowly approved in the Dail, he was telling a cabinet committee, 'that as it now appeared likely, most likely, that there would be bloody rows in Ireland, all orders for withdrawing troops, were to be instantly withdrawn'. In Northern Ireland, Sir James Craig was very nervous as the I.R.A. launched several attacks there. The Treaty had been between Great Britain and the whole of Ireland but the North had the right to opt out, which it exercised. In the South too, the I.R.A. units which did not accept the Treaty, began to take independent action. Churchill felt that British troops might have to assist Collins and Griffith assert their legitimate control. But he ordered the army, 'not to intervene in disturbances without the direct orders of the Viceroy'. On the 14 January, a new Provisional Government came into being in Ireland and undertook to implement the Treaty and assume control from the British. The next day, the seat of British authority in Ireland - Dublin Castle - was handed over to Michael Collins. Churchill began the evacuation of British troops. He also arranged for James Craig and Collins to meet in London. Churchill wrote of this meeting "They both glowered magnificently, but after a short, commonplace talk I slipped away upon some excuse and left them together. What these two Irishmen, separated by such gulfs of religion, sentiment, and conduct, said to each other I cannot tell. But it took a long time, and, as I did not wish to disturb them, mutton chops, etc., were tactfully introduced about one o'clock. At four o'clock the Private Secretary reported signs of movement on the all Ireland front and I ventured to look in. They announced to me complete agreement reduced to writing. They were to help each other in every way; they were to settle outstanding points by personal discussion; they were to stand together within the limits agreed against all disturbances of the peace. We three then joined in the best of all pledges, to wit, 'to try to make things work'.

COLLINS CONNIVES WITH IRA

But those agreements proved difficult to implement as the I.R.A. sometimes with Collins' connivance, continued to launch attacks within the North. There, a huge Protestant, military force was established, paid for by the British Government, but over which, it had no control. The Northern Government had assumed, 'the military functions specially reserved to the British...by simply calling the forces, police'. The North also had the benefit of the direct help of Sir Henry Wilson who was resigning from Government service to become Unionist M.P. for North Down. He helped in the organising of special constabularies,which were exclusively drawn from the Protestant community.

The new Provisional Government was in a very precarious situation, existing bunker like, at Government buildings in Dublin for weeks on end. When Collins made a first visit to his native Cork - the Rebel county - under army escort, shots were fired at one of his public meetings. The headquarters of the Treaty side there, was raided by the I.R.A. and both Collins and his General, Sean MacEoin, were forcedly forbidden to visit the republican plot in the local cemetery. Skirmishes along the border continued with large nationalist areas horrified at being included in the artificial Protestant Unionist state, without any consultation or vote. Churchill felt it would be essential to get arbitration for the Boundary Commission as 'the only way out'. In February he organised a meeting between Collins and Craig in Dublin, but the latter was not willing to give up any territory of the six counties. He informed Lloyd George of this, quoting the 1920 Government of Ireland Act, which set up his State. He also declared that he would not be a party to any Boundary Commission.That same month, I.R.A. units invaded parts of Fermanagh and Tyrone, kidnapping some Unionists. The Northern government sent reinforcements to the border. Winston wrote to his wife who was still on holiday, in the south of France, saying that he would have to keep the Commons in check, during this difficult episode. In the House he said: "We are going to have a very difficult and anxious time, and no man can say with certainty that a good result 'll be achieved, but there is a great hope, that with patience and perseverance we may succeed through all the difficulties of this Irish situation in the same way as, twenty years ago, we found our way through the certainly not less baffling and perplexing difficulties of the South African situation.

At any rate, while there is not the slightest ground for optimism or enthusiasm or vain ebullitions of joy and satisfaction, neither is there the slightest ground in anything that presents itself in any portion of this complicated and difficult Irish situation for weakness, disheartenment, or despair". In Belfast, where Catholics were in a minority and vulnerable, many already under siege were attacked and killed by Protestant mobs.

MARTIAL LAW READY

The Provisional Government intended to have a General Election to seek approval from the electorate for the Treaty. It felt that this was their only way to establish legitimacy. But having an election in the prevailing chaos, was not going to be an easy matter. Churchill was urging the election on Collins and Griffith. But the prospect of an election also gave rise to other fears. General Macready wrote to Churchill as early as 14 February telling him that if DeValera won the election on his republican claim, then he Macready intended immediately to declare martial law. The general also told Winston that if DeValera should stage a coup d'etat before the election was held, then Macready would also impose martial law. He concluded: "If either contingency that I have mentioned should occur, it will be no time for hesitation, and for the sake of the lives of those for whom I am responsible, I shall be obliged to act at once".

Churchill was intent in giving the Provisional Government every help he could, to see that the Treaty was passed by the Commons and implemented on the ground. Speaking on the Second Reading of the Irish Free State Bill he said the Bill 'clothes the Provisional Government with lawful power and enables them to hold an election under favourable conditions at the earliest possible moment...We have never recognised it (a Republic) and never will recognise it... the Republican idea be definitely, finally and completely put aside...(A majority for DeValera would make Ireland) absolutely isolated from the sympathy of the world, bitterly divided in herself in speculating upon these ugly hypotheses".

Churchill had seen Collins for several hours the previous day at the Colonial Office and had assured him of continuing support.In the Commons he continued with customary rhetorical flourish :

PILOTS BILL SETTING UP IRISH FREE STATE

"If you want to see Ireland degenerate into a meaningless welter of lawless chaos and confusion, delay this Bill. If you wish to see increasingly serious bloodshed all along the borders of Ulster, delay this Bill. If you want this House to have on its hands, as it now has, the responsibility for peace and order in southern Ireland, without the means of enforcing it, if you want to impose the same evil conditions upon the Irish Provisional Government, delay this Bill. If you want to enable dangerous and extreme men, working out schemes of hatred and subterranean secrecy, to undermine and overturn a Government which is faithfully doing its best to keep its word with us and enabling us to keep our word with it, delay this Bill. If you want to proclaim to all the world, week after week, that the British Empire can get on just as well without law as with it, then you will delay this Bill.

But if you wish to give a fair chance to a policy to which a Parliament has pledged itself, and to Irish Ministers to whom you are bound in good faith, so long as they act faithfully with you, to give fair play and a fair chance, if you wish to see Ireland brought back from the confusion of tyranny to a reign of law, if you wish to give logical and coherent effect to the policy and experiment to which we are committed, you will not impede, even for a single unnecessary week, the passage of this Bill". Churchill knew that most Conservative anger with the Bill rested then with the Boundary Commission clause which it was envisaged would decrease the territory of the six counties. But he knew it was an essential ingredient of the Treaty. In his speech he reiterated, that in several parts of Fermanagh and Tyrone, "The majority of the inhabitants will prefer to join the Irish Free State... I am not concealing that for a moment. I am locating it, defining it, exposing it. This is the weak point. The Boundary Commission... affects the existing frontiers of Ulster and may conceivably affect them prejudicially... I remember on the eve of the Great War we were gathered together at a cabinet meeting in Downing Street, and for a long time, an hour or an hour and a half, after the failure of the Buckingham Palace conference, we discussed the boundaries of Fermanagh and Tyrone. Both of the great political parties were at each other's throats. The air was full of talk of civil war. Every effort was made to settle and bring them together. The differences had been narrowed down, not merely to the counties of Fermanagh and Tyrone, but to parishes and groups of parishes inside the areas of Fermanagh and Tyrone, and yet, even when the differences had been so narrowed down, the problem seemed to be as insuperable as ever, and neither side would agree to reach any conclusion...

Then came the Great War. Every institution, almost, in the world was strained. Great Empires have been overturned. The whole map of Europe has been changed. The position of countries has been violently altered. The modes of thought of men, the whole outlook on affairs, the grouping of parties, all have encountered violent and tremendous changes in the deluge of the world, but as the deluge subsides and the waters fall short, we see the dreary steeples of Fermanagh and Tyrone emerging once again. The integrity of their quarrel is one of the few institutions that has been unaltered in the cataclysm which has swept the world.

That says a lot for the persistency with which Irish men on one side or the other are able to pursue their controversies. It says a great deal for the power which Ireland has, both Nationalist and Orange, to lay their hands upon the vital strings of British life and politics, and to hold, dominate, and convulse year after year, generation after generation, the politics of this powerful country".

Churchill wanted to reassure those who feared Britain would not defend Ulster against an attack from the South. He said:"Not alone should we defend every inch of Ulster soil under the Treaty as if it were Kent, but we should be bound to take special measures to secure that Ulster was not ruined by her loyalty to us...For generations we have been wandering and floundering in the Irish bog; but at last we think that in this Treaty we have set our feet upon a pathway, which has already become a causeway - narrow, but firm and far-reaching. Let us march along this causeway with determination and circumspection, without losing heart and without losing faith. If Britain continues to march along that path, the day may come - it may be distant but it may not be so distant as we expect - when, turning round, Britain will find at her side Ireland united, a nation, and a friend".

SIR HENRY WILSON WALKS OUT OF COMMONS

Winston's contributions were welcomed by most in the Commons. But the Ulster Unionists and some Tory allies were totally hostile to the clause on the Boundary Commission. Sir Henry Wilson who had only stepped down from being Chief of the Imperial General Staff on 19 February and taken his Commons seat four days later, was foremost in this. The debate went on for days with Winston contributing every day. Sir James Craig put down an amendment rejecting the Boundary Commission but this was defeated by 302 votes to 60. The Bill then went into the Committee Stage where it was dissected for three consecutive days with Winston defending it. On its return to the Chamber again, Sir Henry Wilson was so annoyed with Churchill that he led a walkout as Winston was speaking. Churchill adverted to the international and historical dimensions of the Irish problem as he wound up the debate:

"If you strip Ireland of her grievance, if you strip Ireland of the weapon she has hitherto used, if you strip her of the accusation against Great Britain of being the oppressor, if you strip her of her means of exciting and commanding the sympathy of the whole world, of the support she has received in the United States, in our own Dominions, indeed, throughout the whole English speaking world, if by acting in strict, inflexible good faith you place Ireland in the position that if she breaks the Treaty, she is in the wrong and you are in the right, that she is absolutely isolated in the whole world - then I say, the strength of your economic position emerges in its integrity".

He ended by talking not for the first time in the debate, of how intimately Ireland had been involved in British politics" convulsing parties, disturbing Governments, holding the balance of power for years...But when Ireland is stripped of her grievance and stands on her own resources, then, and then alone, will you know how weak she is, how little power she has to do us harm...Irishmen are capable of producing a Government in their own country, which is not markedly below the standards of the civilisation of Westminster".

During the course of the debate Churchill had received a request from Collins for arms and ammunition. The cabinet committee on Ireland noted that" The Chairman (Churchill), was disposed to issue immediately to the Provisional Government, one thousand rifles and three or four armoured cars, in the clear understanding that that these would not be used on the Border, but only for the purpose of maintaining order in the South". There, violence continued as the anti Treaty and pro Treaty elements of the army jockeyed for position from the departing British forces. People were being killed all over the country. Along the border there was always a possibility that a major shooting war could break out. Churchill wrote to Griffith and Collins urging them to control the I.R.A. He believed that there was no danger of incursions from the North. He assured both men that he was also trying to get Craig to control his forces within the North. In the period January-June 1922, 264 people had been murdered in the North, 171 were Catholic and 93 were Protestant.

SECTARIAN MURDERS IN BELFAST

In late March a shocking sectarian murder of a Catholic family named MacMahon, occurred in Belfast. Churchill felt sure that the British government had to take some action as it paid for the Protestant B Specials, "some of whom had possibly been guilty of these murders. The British Government had a definite responsibility in the matter", he told the Cabinet Committee.

The latter invited Collins and Craig to meet itself. Churchill told the Commons that Craig and Collins had agreed to meet with him. But he was not very hopeful as he said:

"I do not pretend to guarantee that there will be good results from this conference. There may be no result at all, except that both sides may go home with more hopeless feelings than before, and the troubles will continue to grow.

We will do our very best, but it rests with Irishmen who care for Ireland to try to bring about a better state of things. They alone can do it.

Great Britain will help, but the initiative, the controlling administration, has passed out of our hands by our own will, deliberately, into the hands of Irishmen. Let them meet together, and endeavour to create in a satisfactory manner a decent future for Ireland". Collins and Craig arrived in London the next morning.Collins had a picture with him of the murdered MacMahon family, which he showed to Churchill, who wept at the sight. That afternoon Collins sat in the distinguished visitors Gallery of the Commons to hear Churchill speak of the horrible deeds being perpetrated in Belfast. He said:

"I think one would have to search all over Europe to find instances of equal atrocity, barbarity, cold blooded, inhuman, cannibal vengeance - cannibal in all except the act of devouring the flesh of the victim...We seek only the repression and the termination of these horrors. We have no other object and no other interest. The rest must lie with the representatives of the Irish people across the Channel. Everything we can do to help them to shake themselves free from this convulsion and spasm - due no doubt to the tragedies of the past - will be done, and every action which I shall submit from this box must be defended and justified only in reference to that".

COLLINS - CRAIG AGREEMENT

Churchill prepared a draft agreement between Northern Ireland and the South for the first meeting in London between Collins, Griffith, Duggan, Kevin O'Higgins and James Craig and Lord Londonderry. A Conference took place at Churchill's Colonial Office over two days. The basis of the draft was finally agreed to, despite many difficulties raised by Kevin O'Higgins in particular. Craig offended many of his own supporters by attending this meeting, but part of his strategy was to ingratiate himself with Churchill, on whom he largely depended. The Heads of Agreement between the governments said :

"1. Peace is declared today.

2. From today the two governments undertake to cooperate in every way in their power with a view to the restoration of peaceful conditions in the unsettled areas..

3. ...in Belfast... special police in mixed districts to be composed of half of Catholics and half of Protestants...all specials not required for this force to be withdrawn to their homes and their arms handed in...

6. I.R.A. activity to cease in the Six Counties...

10. The two Governments...shall arrange for the release of political prisoners...".

On the following day Winston read the agreement to the Commons. He hoped it would finish "the religious and partisan warfare in Belfast itself and the acts of repeated injury and counter-injury which have been done to Catholics and Protestants, one against the other. There will be forces in Ireland anxious to wreck these arrangements by violent action, by treacherous action, and, if possible, to throw suspicion upon the good faith of those with whom we have entered into a covenant. We must be prepared in our minds for that...". The Northern Nationalist M.P.,

Joseph Devlin, spoke of Churchill's endeavours. He said, "May I also be allowed to congratulate the right honourable gentleman on the superb tact and ability with which he has conducted all these Irish matters since he has been entrusted with this task". The Bill recognising the Treaty became law that same day. The King sent a message to Winston:"... must congratulate you upon the successful conclusion of a difficult and responsible task, thanks to the skill, patience, tact, which you have displayed in handling it and for which you have earned universal gratitude".

WINSTON TAKES FAMILY TO CHARTWELL

It was at this time that Winston decided to take the family down to Kent to see his new interest - Chartwell, the house and estate which he was still planning to buy. He suggested a picnic in the country as a rouse, so that Clementine would not be suspicious. They drove down and set up their table outside the empty house. He asked the children what they thought of the place. They loved it. He asked the four months pregnant Clementine what she thought of it. She replied that it was quite nice. Then he announced that he had bought it (though the deal was not to be finalised until the following September). His wife was horrified as she realised that there would be enormous renovation and upkeep costs. She thought it would require fourteen servants to run it properly. He told her not to worry so much about that aspect of it. Mary, with whom Clementine was then pregnant, said later that her father used to say of Chartwell, that a day spent away from the place, was for him, a day wasted. But though it was to be their home for the next forty years, Clementine never had any great feel for the place. She accepted it as a fait accompli and got to work with Winston, making it an acceptable place to live.

CHAPTER 11

SECURING THE PEACE

Unfortunately, the recently signed agreement between the two parts of Ireland had little affect in stopping the violence within the North. Collins felt that the Catholics there were still being victimised and he continued to collaborate with the I.R.A. there. He also ensured that various government departments did not cooperate with their opposites in the North. He was basically still trying to ensure that there would be a meeting of minds between the pro and anti Treaty elements. This did not make Craig's serious attempts to honour the Pact easy, as he was being pressurised by his own hardliners.

It was within the South that the Provisional Government had its main concerns. A Convention of the I.R.A. repudiated its authority and that of its National army. The I.R.A. controlled many parts of the South and vowed its allegiance to the 'Republic'. Churchill feared that the I.R.A. might declare a Republic and take over the South. He told the cabinet committee that Britain would not stand for that. He made plans to blockade such a 'republic' into submission.

At the Easter adjournment debate in the Commons, Lord Robert Cecil criticised the Government's handling of Ireland. He particularly mentioned the atrocities of the Black and Tans. Churchill then was put into the position of defending them, which in the contemporary situation was to say the least, unfortunate. He said: "Everyone knows that armed men will not stand by and see one after another of their number shot down by treachery, without to some extent taking the law into their own hands.Although the government did their best to restrain them, it is perfectly true that we did not punish with full severity persons who had been mixed up in this sort of affair. We have never concealed that.How could we punish them while there was no other redress open to them, while no court would convict, while no criminals were arrested, while there was no means whatever of affording these men the satisfaction of a sense of self-preservation, when they saw comrades weltering in blood from a foul blow?".

Churchill told the Cabinet several times of his fears of the Republicans, against whom Collins seemed reluctant to move. He said that Collins and Griffith felt it vital and indispensable to the success of the Treaty, to avoid striking the first blow against Republicans. He told Lloyd George that he was passing up a ten day painting holiday on the Riviera, where he went regularly, to stay in London for the Easter. He hoped that the Provisional Government would come good. On 12 April he wrote a personal letter to Collins urging him to put his case to the Irish people, before the country was further ruined. He wrote;

"The Cabinet instructed me to send you a formal communication expressing their growing anxiety at the spread of disorder in the twenty six counties. Instead of this, however, I write to you as man to man. Many residents are writing to this country tales of intimidation, disorder, theft and pillage. There is no doubt that capital is taking flight. Credits are shutting up, railways are slowing down, business and enterprise are baffled. The wealth of Ireland is undergoing a woeful shrinkage. Up to a certain point no doubt these facts may have the beneficial effect of rousing all classes to defend their own material interests, and Mr. DeValera may gradually come to personify not a cause, but a catastrophe. It is difficult for us over here to measure truly, but it is obvious that in the long run the Government, however patient, must assert itself or perish and be replaced by some other form of control. Surely the moment will come when you can broadly and boldly appeal not to any clique, sect or faction, but to the Irish nation as a whole. They surely have a right to expect you to lead them out of the dark places, and the opportunity is one (the loss of) which history will never forgive. Ought you not to rally round the infant Free State all the elements in Ireland which will wholeheartedly adhere to the Treaty and sign a declaration attaching them to it, irrespective of what their former attitudes have been? Would you not find reserves on this basis infinitely more powerful than any you have obtained at the present time? Ought you not to summon your 'far flung people' to your aid? In America, Australia, Canada, New Zealand, there must be hundreds of Irishmen intensely devoted to the welfare and freedom of their native land, who would come to see fair play over the elections and make sure that the people had a fair vote.

Every day that the uncertainty continues must be attended by the progressive impoverishment of Ireland. Nobody can invest or make plans for production, while the threat of civil war, or of a Republic followed by a state of war with the British Empire, hangs over the country. I trust the end of May, or at the very latest, the first week in June, will see the issue submitted to the Irish people. We really have a moral right to ask you that the uncertainty as to whether our offer is accepted or rejected should not be indefinitely prolonged...".

IRA TAKE OVER FOUR COURTS

The very next day, the I.R.A. in Dublin, took over the important and central Four Courts complex, less than one mile from the seat of Government. It displayed the contempt in which it held the Provisional Government and its creator and mentor, the British government. Chaos seemed to have finally arrived. The I.R.A., under Rory O'Connor, took its mandate from the Volunteer Convention of 26 March, which repudiated the new Government. On 9 April the I.R.A. "declared itself independent of civilian authority, assumed all responsibility for public order, and proposed to postpone elections, ' while the threat of war with England exists". DeValera, though also repudiated by this group of militant I.R.A. people, made speeches which seemed to incite a civil war. DeValera and Collins had an agreement from January to postpone elections for three months. Churchill well realised the complex manipulations for power going on between the two ex-comrades. DeValera wished to keep off elections for as long as possible, as he knew the Treaty would be backed by the electorate. Churchill tried to work against DeValera, advising Collins to have the elections early, thereby getting the terms of the Treaty accepted.

Churchill was pleased by reports from General Macready and Alfred Cope, Irish Secretary, saying that the Irish people were coming more and more to support the Provisional government and that the occupation of the Four Courts was proving counter productive. These two British officials advised that Collins was right, for the moment, not to attack the complex. Churchill continued to supply the new Government with arms and ammunition. He again suggested that another meeting between Craig and Collins should be held. He wrote to Collins on 29 April, warning him that his opponents in the North hoped for a Republic, knowing that it would come into direct conflict with the Empire. Winston said that Collins' opponents in the South hoped to see him defeated by ongoing chaos in the North. He advised Collins to treat the North carefully, pointing out that casualties were occurring on both sides. He said that Britain stood by the Treaty and the Irish people should be allowed to vote on the matter.

CHURCHILL FEARS BETRAYAL

Two weeks later, Churchill was furious to discover that DeValera and Collins were negotiating an electoral pact, to put a united front to the electorate, which would not alter the existing groupings within the Dail. "The Irish terrorists are naturally drawn to imitate Lenin and Trotsky: while we should take our stand on the will of the people freely expressed" he said. This alignment between the hated republican DeValera and the Provisional Government would put in jeopardy all of Winston's strategies. He wrote bitterly to Collins:

"I think I had better let you know at once that any such arrangement would be received with world-wide ridicule and reprobation. It would not be an election in any sense of the word, but simply a farce, were a handful of men who possess lethal weapons deliberately to dispose of the political rights of the electors, by a deal across the table. Such an arrangement would not strengthen your own position in the slightest degree. It would not invest the Provisional Government with any title to sit in the name of the Irish nation. It would be an outrage upon democratic principles and would be universally so denounced.

Your Government would soon find itself regarded as a tyrannical junta which having got into office by violence, was seeking to maintain itself by a denial of constitutional rights. The enemies of Ireland have been accustomed to say that the Irish people did not care about representative government, that it was alien to their instincts, and that if they had an opportunity they would return to a despotism or oligarchy in one form or another. If you were to allow yourself to be misled into such an arrangement as is indicated, such action would be immediately proclaimed as justifying to the full this sinister prediction. As far as we are concerned in this country, we should certainly not be able to regard any such arrangement as a basis on which we could build".The next day Winston told the Cabinet that the Irish leaders 'had been men of violence and conspiracy and had hardly emerged from that atmosphere'. An election pact would again give 64 pro Treaty members and 57 anti Treaty members. A Cabinet of five of the former and four of the latter groupings would be formed. The anti-Treaty ministers intended to revoke the Treaty and abandon the Crown.

Sir James Craig took this opportunity to successfully ask Churchill for extra arms to guard the border. He also declared that his Government would accept no changes on the border, despite what any Boundary Commission might find. This declaration infuriated Winston as he had just got the Provisional government to agree to meet him in London. He felt that if Craig could snub the Imperial Government, the people from the South would do likewise.

In London Griffith and Collins told Churchill that a successful election in the South needed Republican approval. Otherwise they said, it might easily be disrupted. But they promised to hold the election in June. They also assured Winston that, despite the election pact with DeValera, they would still emerge victorious and implement the Treaty. Winston ended their discussion with some stern words saying:

"There has been a great change of opinion in this country. We made a big concession to you in the shape of the Free State. We said 'No Republic', but you have made one surrender after another to the Republicans and have not obtained the free opinion of the Irish people. The result is that in this country there is fierce scrutiny of our actions. You will find that we are just as tenacious on essential points - the Crown, the British Commonwealth, no Republic - as DeValera and Rory O'Connor, and we intend to fight for our points".

But Churchill accepted their assurances and backed them in cabinet, saying, "some Labour and Independent candidates might be elected, and Mr. Collins has received assurances that after the Election, some of DeValera's supporters would cross over, because they were convinced that England was loyally carrying out her pledges. The idea was to try and get a non-Party Government, so as to secure tranquility in Ireland, and at a later stage a proper Election on the main issue". Collins had visions of forming a Constitutional Assembly as a first step towards peace.

Churchill was also concerned about the dangers of further trouble on the border. He told the same cabinet meeting: "The two Governments were further apart from each other than ever, and each blamed the other. Sir James Craig blamed the supporters of DeValera... and Collins admitted this. Since the breaching of the Pact and a boycotting of Northern goods in the South, and other measures, the I.R.A. had become more effective. Whether it was a case of six of one and half a dozen of the other, he did not know. He would be sorry to arrive at any other ratio. The border was in a dangerous situation, and matters were worse in Belfast than they had been...".

CHURCHILL ARMS THE NORTH

Despite his apparent even handed approach, Winston had no doubt but that they had to send massive arms shipments to

Ulster. He was also ready to envisage direct British assistance to the North. He believed the troubles within the north were due to "two so-called divisions of the I.R.A. located in Ulster". He felt that the Specials should be extended to 48,000 and the British army to 9,000. He told the Cabinet:

"We could do no less... the ferocious steps used against Ulster...Collins having joined with avowed republicans".

He continued: "Ministers should read the Irish papers, such as the 'Freeman'. These papers, published in Dublin - and they are pro-Treaty papers - describe only the murders of Catholics and attribute these horrors to Sir James Craig's Government and the Orangemen. Every outrage on one side is replied to by an outrage on the other in a crescendo of conflict which may bring about an explosion, which may put an end to our watching the laboured processes connected with the Constitution".

Collins and Griffith convinced Churchill that their Agreement with DeValera need not inhibit the successful holding of the Election

The next day in the Commons, Winston said that the DeValera-Collins election pact could provide a cessation of all attacks on Ulster by the I.R.A., to a cessation of the murder of ex-servants of the Crown, of the murder of Protestants in the South, and of ex-British soldiers. He hoped the Election would lead to a Constitution linking Ireland firmly to the Crown and Empire. "I do not believe" he said, "that (the Provisional Government) are working hand in glove with their Republican opponents with the intent, by an act of treachery, to betray British confidence and Ireland's good name. We have transferred the powers of Government...to the Irish Parliament. We have done this on the faith of the Treaty...This great act of faith on the part of the stronger power, will not, I believe, be brought to mockery by the Irish people. If it were, the strength of the Empire will survive the disappointment, but the Irish name will not soon recover from the disgrace". Sir Henry Wilson again led the opposition to Churchill, asking "can we wait while men are murdered?". Herbert Asquith was full of praise for Winston's stance. Among the visitors at the House that day were Collins and Griffith.

That same day in the North occurred an event which could have upset all the plans of the politicians. A group of armed men took over the villages of Pettigo and Beleek on the Border. Craig quickly informed Churchill, who told Lloyd George. The two Irish leaders were invited to ten Downing St., where they assured the P.M. that they were not involved in the action. Collins later, went to see Winston at the Colonial Office, where he was more keen to discuss Winstons' speech in the Commons than the Pettigo incident. Some days later Churchill wrote to Collins in lightly concealed anger:

"On Wednesday last information was received that armed republican forces had invaded the Northern territory and had entered Beleek and Pettigo... We immediately brought this to your notice...you told us that these forces were not your forces and you disclaimed any responsibility for them. I announced this in Parliament.

It is with surprise that I received in the Communique issued from the G.H.Q. Beggars Bush that there were 'no other Irish troops than our troops "i.e. Free State Troops" in the district now or then". I shall be glad if you will explain this discrepancy".

The Irish delegation had come to London with their Draft Constitution. The British were aghast at its republicanism. Discussions went on for almost a week while the British tried to get it changed. Once more Winston found himself making preparations least Ireland declare a Republic. He told the Cabinet of a plan to starve Ireland of cash, by stopping the collection of revenue by the Provisional Government. The discussions dragged on for a second week until on 15 June

Winston announced to the Commons that agreement was reached. The British were finally happy that the new Constitution be put to the Irish electorate on the following day. It said the Irish Free State would be 'a co-equal member of the community of nations forming the British Commonwealth of Nations: the King would be the Head of the State Legislature'.

PETTIGO-BELEEK INCIDENT WORSENS

While agreement on the Constitution was being discussed, the incident at Pettigo-Beleek continued to unfold. Were it not for the overlordship of Lloyd George, the natural impetuosity of Churchill might have caused a major break with the Irish over what was a rather minor event. The republican force was still occupying the area. Churchill gave orders for British troops to surround the area by entering the Free State and attacking from there. Seven of the republicans were killed in the action at Pettigo. Collins, who had returned to Dublin, asked Churchill to cease the intrusion into the Free State and the military action at Beleek Castle, which was also in the Free State. Collins called the British action an "unwarrantable interference with our forces in our territory" adding that the action could become "disastrous" and "imperil the whole situation". Alfred Cope wrote to Thomas Jones that the barracks at Pettigo was occupied by Free State soldiers who had not fired on the British army and "any firing from the South...must have been the work of irregulars". Cope believed that the British troops "hit the wrong people". Collins demanded an inquiry into the whole business.

LLOYD GEORGE CHIDES WINSTON'S IMPETUOSITY

As usual Winston was taken with any military activity and was not anxious to cease until he was completely victorious. Lloyd

George was very concerned least the incident cause a wider conflagration. He asked the cabinet secretary to talk to Winston, who did not enjoy being checked on. Jones reported on his meeting with Winston that the latter 'was most anxious that I should put the business in as favourable a light as possible'. Jones of course was a powerful individual with the ear of the P.M. as Cabinet secretary. His record of the meeting is a fascinating account, showing Winston as still, the little boy who resented any other boy interfering with his game. Jones' record of the meeting is: "The conversation became more and more personal. I said now that the Treaty had been put through, I felt less biased in favour of the South. We had put ourselves right and the important thing was to be absolutely fair as between the North and South. Why was not pressure brought on Craig to deal with the murderers in Belfast? Churchill said he was doing so and that he had to try to retain the confidence of the Ulster people in him and he had to watch our Parliamentary position: that he could not face Parliament on Monday, if he were unable to say what the position in a British village was. I said I recognised the great patience he had shown up to the present in dealing with the Irish situation, but that I was very nervous about impulsive action with the troops. He said if the P.M. was going to butt in, he could take the business on himself and have his resignation".

Churchill stood his ground and sent a letter with Jones to the P.M. telling him of other military action which was pending:

"The troops having taken Pettigo, are now preparing to move forward on Beleek village. This is wholly in our territory,and we certainly cannot allow it to remain in the hands of raiders". The very next morning Collins and Griffith were due back in London with a revised Draft Constitution. Lloyd George realised that Churchill's planned military action could wreck everything. He decided that he had to be careful though decisive with Winston, who might resign over being countermanded. He wrote a letter with great care in case Winston might later use the letter against him. He also sent a copy of it to the King, who was on excellent terms with Winston. Lloyd George wrote sternly:

"I am profoundly disquieted by the developments on the Ulster border. We are not merely being rushed into a conflict, but we are gradually being manoeuvred into giving battle on the very worst grounds which could possibly be chosen for the struggle. I cannot say whether Henry Wilson and DeValera are behind this, but if they are their strategy is very skilful. They both want a break and they both want to fight a battle on this ground. I am not convinced that a break is inevitable. On the contrary, with patience, with the adroitness of which you have such command, I believe we can get through in the end...Ulster divides British opinion at home and throughout the Empire. It consolidates American opinion against us. The same thing applies to French, Italian and Belgium opinion. But if the Free Staters insisted on a Constitution which repudiated Crown and Empire and practically set up a republic, we could carry the whole world with us in any action we took. That is why the Anti-Treaty-ites are forcing the issue on Ulster.

Moreover, our Ulster case is not a good one;

(1) We have 9,000 troops in Ulster and we are half maintaining and wholly equipping another force of 48,000 Specials... in two years 400 Catholics have been killed and 1,200 wounded without a single person being brought to justice.

(2) It is true that several Protestants have also been murdered... It must be also be noticed that no Catholic has been arrested. This is a comment on the criticism directed against the Free State, because the murderers of 37 Protestants have been arrested in that area.

(3) It was reported to us on the authority, I believe, of the Ulster Government that there were concentrations of Free State troops against Londonderry, Strabane and the Pettigo salient and a serious invasion predicted. On investigation it was discovered that there were no troops massing against either Londonderry or Strabane. When we got to the Pettigo salient and threatened it by an elaborate manoeuvre with two brigades of infantry and one battery of artillery, we found twenty three Free Staters on Free State territory in Pettigo, of whom seven were killed and fifteen captured. If war comes out of this, will it not make us rather ridiculous?"

Lloyd George then could not resist introducing a note of ridicule for Winston's discomfort. He went on:

(4) Now I understand we are marching against some rotten barrack at Beleek, garrisoned by a friendly blacksmith and a handful of his associates with an equally formidable force.

The P.M. then referred to General Sean MacEoin, the commander of the Free State army, who "is a very strong Treaty man and has publicly denounced DeValera and the pact. If he should be killed at Beleek, it would be a disaster to the cause of reconciliation with the Irish race. Please bear that in mind. Quite frankly if we force the issue with these facts, we shall be hopelessly beaten...Let us keep on the high ground of the Treaty - the Crown, the Empire. There we are unassailable. But if you come down from that height and fight in the swamps of Lough Erne, you will be overwhelmed".

After setting out such unpalatable home truths to Winston, the P.M. felt it would be politic to massage his large ego, before he warned him against further foolish military actions.

He continued: "You have conducted these negotiations with such skill and patience, that I beg you not to be tempted into squandering what you have already gained by a precipitous action, however alluring the immediate prospect may be. We have surely done everything that Ulster can possibly expect to ensure its security. Fifty seven thousand armed men ought to be equal to the protection of so small a territory. If they require more they can get them. But if we indulge in provocative action on the frontier, incidents will be inevitable. It is our business as a great Empire to be strictly impartial in our attitude towards all creeds. We have more creeds assembled under our Flag than any empire in the world and our prestige depends upon maintaining a stern impartiality in our attitude towards them".

This letter tells us how well Lloyd George understood Winston's impetuosity in military matters. It also shows us that Winston learned little caution from the Dardanelles fiasco. The fact that the P.M. was so careful in his handling of the letter demonstrates how suspicious of Winston he was. It is very ironic to hear the great imperialist tutored in political imperialism. The use of the term 'creed' in the latter part of the letter may lend some credence to those who claim that Churchill saw the Irish conflict as between Catholics and Protestants, and always acted accordingly.

That very same evening the incident at Beleek ended peacefully, when the soldiers occupying the Fort left, and it and Beleek were occupied by the British. Winston, hurt by Lloyd George's rebuff, wrote to Austen Chamberlain saying that the interaction of the local and general situation had been very worrying, but he didn't think any harm had been done.

Collins confirmed Churchill's faith in him by agreeing to constitutional changes which would give the King the formalities of executive power in the Irish Free State, and make any constitutional changes, conflicting with the Treaty, void. These changes were not to be published until the early hours of the forthcoming election day. As Collins shook Churchill's hand before they parted in London,he said prophetically, "I shall not last long. My life's forfeit, but I'll do my best. After I'm gone it will be easier for others. You'll find they will be able to do more than I can do". Churchill understood the gravity of the statement and could only stammer, "All will come right".

The General Election results in Ireland showed as expected, that the Provisional Government carried the day very well, despite the DeValera-Collins Pact, which didn't take effect. The Labour Party, which was pro-Treaty, made unexpected gains and Labour voters transferred their later preferences to the pro-Treaty party. But the I.R.A. was still in a very powerful position around the country, rejecting the Treaty, the Partition of the country and the legitimate Government. The new Government now had fifty eight members to thirty five for the opposition. Winston had been vindicated. Collins and Griffith assurances to him had proved to be correct. DeValera had lost out badly.

SIR HENRY WILSON ASSASSINATED

But at the same time as these election results were being announced, came the shattering news from London, that Sir Henry Wilson had been assassinated outside his Eaton Place home. Two Irishmen were apprehended. They claimed that they had acted alone due to Wilson's attitude to Ireland. But a note found on one of them seemed to indicate that other murders were planned. Wilson's murder was probably ordered by Michael Collins. A wave of anti-Irish feeling again swept over England, all but engulfing Churchill and the others in government. The Conservative element of the Government, which was by far the largest, was only barely tolerating the Treaty with the Irish. The Cabinet were infuriated and frightened as Winston laid the fatal weapon on the table in front of them. They each got police protection.The Cabinet decided that the time had come for them to insist that the Government in Dublin take steps against the I.R.A.. In particular it wanted action at the Four Courts, 'from which are believed to emanate the principal plots in Southern Ireland, in Northern Ireland and in the U.K., and where it is reported considerable armaments, including guns are stored'. Winston was instructed to draw up a letter which would be sent immediately to Collins.

BRITISH ULTIMATUM TO COLLINS

The letter was sent the same evening. It read :

"Dear Mr. Collins, I am desired by His Majesty's Government to inform you that documents have been found upon the murderers of Sir Henry Wilson which clearly connect the assassins with the Irish Republican Army, and which further reveal the existence of a definite conspiracy against the peace and order of this country...The ambiguous position of the I.R.A. can no longer be ignored by the British Government. Still less can Rory O'Connor be permitted to remain with his followers and his arsenal in open rebellion in the heart of Dublin in possession of the Courts of Justice, organising and sending out from this centre enterprises of murder...His Majesty's Government cannot consent to a continuance of this state of things, and they feel entitled to ask you formally to bring it to an end forthwith...are prepared to place at your disposal the necessary pieces of artillery". The letter was signed by Lloyd George. That night Churchill slept in the attic of his house with a Colt automatic at his side. He had an armchair in the room reinforced with metal, behind which he intended to take cover as he fought with any intruders. It did not seem to cross his mind that any would-be assassins might not be aware that his wife slept alone and mistake her in the dark for their real target. She did not appear to be very worried about the prospect of any attack.

General Macready informed the Cabinet that he had a plan ready to take the Four Courts with British troops, should Collins refuse to act. Churchill drafted a top secret Proclamation 'to the citizens of Dublin' in the event of the British taking direct action. He also sent ships to Dublin capable of holding 400 prisoners. Churchill's plan was to attack the Four Courts on Sunday 25 June, after Collins' reply did not offer immediate action. But Macready decided that a Sunday was not a good day for an attack, as ironically most of the garrison of the Four Courts 'went away for the weekend'. This was quite true as one of the officers, Sean MacBride, has told of how their operation was in some respects an informal one, with both sides having an understanding that they would not attack one another. MacBride has told of going for drives in the country on Sundays and visiting girlfriends or their homes for the weekends. Macready also claimed that a three day notice of military action would be required by the Irish government. He further said that precipitate action by the British might be the catalyst to bring 'the two wings of the I.R.A. together'. He countenanced caution.

The next day saw the State funeral of Henry Wilson at St. Paul's Cathedral where the tension was very great, with much animosity directed towards Churchill and the Government. In the afternoon a debate on Ireland began in the Commons. Winston was the main Government speaker. He first paid tribute to Henry Wilson. He then traced events since the Treaty was signed. He attacked DeValera as the principal wrecker trying to prevent the Irish people from accepting the Treaty. He next turned his attention to the 'so-called I.R.A.' using words which have become all too common and apposite in the intervening years. "The Irish Republican Army was an association of persons for the purpose of organising attacks upon the Crown forces, ranging from individual murders up to considerable ambuscades. It is not capable, and has not at any time been capable, of fighting any serious action according to the rules of war. Nevertheless, it contains a considerable number of men perfectly ready to suffer imprisonment and execution for what they consider to be their cause...". Speaking of the North Winston said:

"Every outrage by the I.R.A. was repaid with bloody interest. Provocation, reprisals, and counterreprisals have now built up a ghastly score on both sides, in which, no doubt, the Catholics, being numerically weaker, have got the worst of it, and have suffered about double as many casualties as the Protestants". He then laid the major blame for this on the actions of the I.R.A. for trying to coerce Ulster into the South. He spoke of a plan to neutralise a zone along the border, which had the approval of Collins and Craig. He said that peace was the only way to unity:

"The greedy and criminal design of breaking down the North, either by disorder from within, or by incursion from without, has got to die in the hearts of those who nourish it...The Sinn Fein Party has got to realise, once and for all, that they will never win Ulster, except by her own free will, and that the more that they kick against the pricks, the worse it will be for them".

He then spoke of the I.R.A. occupation of the Four Courts and issued a Government ultimatum: "If it does not come to an end...His Majesty's Government shall regard the Treaty as having been formally violated...and we shall resume full liberty of action in any direction...".

Chapter 12

FOUNDER OF THE IRISH FREE STATE

Despite Churchill's threats in the Commons, General Macreadys advice to act cautiously was adhered to by the cabinet. This proved to be the correct strategy. Though the standoff between the I.R.A. within the Four Courts and the national army without, was part comical and part collaborative, it was real and always bore the seeds of a tragic finale. Everyone knew that if the complex was attacked that would herald the start of a civil war all over the country. This was precisely what Michael Collins had been maneouvering to avoid at all costs. A few days after the Commons ultimatum, the Assistant Chief of Staff of the Free State Army, Ginger O'Connell, was kidnapped by elements within the Four Courts, as a reprisal for the capture of one of their men. O'Connell was kept prisoner within the Court complex. The Provisional Government decided that it then had acceptable reason to take drastic action. It served notice on the illegal occupiers of the complex to evacuate and surrender, or else the necessary military action would be taken at once. The army surrounded the complex. They had got two eighteen-pounder guns from Macrready via Churchill. The attack began on 28 June. After several hours of shelling they ran out of ammunition. Macready was reluctant to supply more ammunition. Collins telegraphed Winston saying, 'imperative that our further requirements should be met tonight without fail'. Winston told Collins that help would be forthcoming and that the British would finish the job ' if you feel you can carry it no further'. Alfred Cope advised that it would be 'fatal' for the British army to become involved. The British handed over four eighteen pounders and two sixty pounders with three hundred high explosive shells. Churchill also offered to provide aeroplanes, if required. At an I.R.A. Convention two months earlier, Rory O'Connor 's group had argued,without success for an all out attack on the remaining British forces.

The attack on the Four Courts was inevitable as the people there represented an element which would not accept the democratic will of the people. Unfortunately there were many more of like mind throughout the country, often dividing father against son or brother against brother. One of the Fourt Courts garrison from the beginning was Sean MacBride. On the day it was attacked, his mother Maud Gonne MacBride was in Paris, representing the Free State Government at an international forum. She had accepted the Treaty initially, at least, while her son had rejected it. Nevertheless news of the attack was greeted with shock, as all knew what it heralded.

In the Commons Churchill said:

"The Provisional Government and the troops under their orders... are making an effort and they are suffering, and it is quite true of both sides that there is little organisation. Both sides are weak, but it is certainly not a time to mock at a serious attempt made by men who are striking a blow for freedom, order and ultimately unity of their country". DeValera said that those in the Four Courts were 'the best and bravest of our nation. In Rory O'Connor and his comrades lives the unbought and indomitable soul of Ireland'. The next day DeValera himself enlisted as a volunteer in the I.R.A.

CIVIL WAR LOOMS

The Four Courts soon became a burning inferno and its republican garrison surrendered. Many of Ireland's most treasured historical records were destroyed, eliciting from Churchill the felicitious but unfeeling comment: 'better a State without an archive than an archive without a State'. Thirty Free State soldiers had been killed in the action. Other battles took place around the city during which the new recruit DeValera, though surrounded by the Free State army, escaped capture. The Government issued a Proclamation saying it would deal severally with republican activists. It appealed for recruits for the national army. The I.R.A. were quickly driven out of most towns and cities as the army recruiting brought its strength up to 55,000 men within nine months.

The British believed that at last, the Treaty was being safeguarded. Churchill had understood the difficulties but also hoped for the future as he wrote to Collins on 7 July: "...I feel this has been a terrible ordeal for you and your colleagues...the action was indispensable... I could not have sustained another debate in the House of Commons...the Treaty would have fallen...from the Imperial point of view there is nothing we should like better than to see North and South join hands in an all-Ireland assembly without prejudice to the existing rights of either...the Union of South Africa was achieved on a wave of impulse...prejudices die hard...even a month or two may produce enormous changes in public opinion...I hope you are taking good care of yourself and your colleagues, the times are very dangerous".

Winston also wrote to Sir James Craig that same day:
"...I always live in hopes that we may come back again to your suggestion of the Craig-Collins pact to stand together and

settle the outstanding differences in accord...all the more possible now that you seem to be getting increasing control of the situation in Ulster and now that Collins has definitely drawn the sword". Churchill told Craig that through cooperation it might be possible to "render the intervention of the Boundary Commission unnecessary".

In the South the Irish Labour Party had tried to call a meeting of all members of the Dail to discuss peace. Churchill opposed this as it could 'only encourage the rebels, prolong the fight and increase the destruction of property'.

COLLINS PROTESTS ABOUT NORTH

Despite the impending war in the South, Collins still watched developments in the North. On 28 June he wrote to Churchill condemning the decision there to end proportional representation in local government elections. He said:

"the grave effect of this Bill on Nationalist thought in Ulster and in general all over the country, coupled with Sir James Craig's attitude on the Boundary Commission, cannot be exaggerated.

Safeguards for the minority under our jurisdiction have been frequently demanded and readily granted by us. Our people in the North are not slow to notice this, and continually put it to us that their rights under the Craig regime, are not protected in the slightest degree...The effect of this enactment will be to wipe out completely all effective representation of Catholic and Nationalist interest. The Nationalist strongholds of County Fermanagh, County Tyrone, Derry City, as well as several urban and rural districts will go and completely anti-Catholic juntas, will reign in their place.

You will agree, I am sure that nothing could be more detrimental to the cause of peace".

On 9 August again Collins wrote to Churchill condemning the gerrymandering of local government constituencies:

"Do you not see...the true meaning of all this? Not merely is it intended to oust the Catholic and Nationalist people of the Six Counties from their rightful share in local administration, but it is, beyond all question, intended to paint the Counties of Tyrone and Fermanagh with a deep Orange tint in anticipation of the operation of the Boundary Commission, and so, to try to defraud these people of the benefits of the Treaty".

Due to the objections of the Provisional Government, Royal Assent for this Bill was withheld until September. Churchill insisted on some minor concessions, which Craig went along with adhering to his policy of, "no issue should arise publicly upon which it could be urged by those with whom he had to work with in the North, that either he had scored a personal success over Her Majesty's Government or, alternatively, he had given way weakly to HMG". Despite some early efforts to give Catholics a role in the new State, Craig decided that his fundamental role was to respond to his own Unionist pressures.

Unfortunately for succeeding generations, the British government decided to wash its hands of internal affairs in the North, and no act of generosity was possible between the two beleagured groupings there, rather the contrary occurred.

ARTHUR GRIFFITH AND MICHAEL COLLINS DEAD

A few days later Arthur Griffith died in a Dublin hospital, exhausted from the terrible ordeal of the last few years. Churchill felt his death was a "serious blow. But I think we are strong enough now to survive. Poor fellow, he was a man of good faith and good will. I wish he had not died'. Clementine Churchill thought him 'the one decent man they had to represent them'. She wished to send a wreath from herself and Winston.

Michael Collins bearing the coffin of Arthur Griffith, who died in August 1922, flanked by Michael Hayes, Speaker of the Third Dáil, and J.J. Walsh, Minister for Posts and Telegraphs. Collins, who was Chief of Staff of the Free State forces, was killed in an ambush at Béal na Bláth, Co. Cork, the same month.

Ten days later, on 22 August, an armoured Free State column was ambushed in county Cork and Michael Collins was shot dead by the I.R.A. He had only recently sent word to Winston; "Tell Winston we could never have done without him". The deaths of the two main signatories of the Treaty was a very unsettling development for the British and the fledgling Provisional Government. Winston worried least a realignment take place which would give DeValera any power. But there was little chance of that. In fact the death of Collins removed the main conciliating force at the cabinet and inevitably hardened the role of the survivors.

IRISHMEN WHOSE WORD IS THEIR BOND

William T. Cosgrave, a forty two year old civilian, was the cabinet's choice as the new Irish leader. Cosgrave had an impeccable revolutionary record, having been at the inaugural meeting of Sinn Fein in 1905. He took part in the 1916 Rising and the subsequent Anglo-Irish war. He had hesitated before accepting the Treaty but once the decision was made, he was adamant that the forces of democracy would win out over those who opposed it with arms. As early as 24 August, at the instigation of Cope, Churchill wrote to Cosgrave on the importance of a continuity of policy

"...the death of the two principal signatories, the retirement of another and the desertion of the fourth, in no way affect the validity and sanctity of the settlement...between the two islands which was the life- work of the dead Irish leaders, and with which their names will be imperishably associated...You may count on the fullest measure of co-operation and support from us in any way that is required".

Churchill also wrote to Cope advising him of how to proceed with the new leaders, but above all to ensure that DeValera remained "a hunted rebel". He wrote: "The danger to be avoided is a sloppy accomodation with a quasi-repentant DeValera... rebel leaders ought to be rigorously shut out". Winston was later to remark that in Cosgrave, Mulcahy and O'Higgins, 'we have found Irishmen whose word is their bond'. Cosgrave spoke in the Dail on 12 September saying that all arms must be surrendered. He said the Treaty would be honoured and the new Constitution would be ready for British parliamentary ratification before 6 December, on which date, under the Treaty, the authority of the Provisional Government ceased. Ratification would mean the legal establishment of the Irish Free State.

Cosgrave like Collins was concerned at events in the North as proportional representation came to be abolished. He too wrote to Churchill because "it was not a 'domestic matter' for Northern Ireland and it loads the dice against the Free State before the Boundary Commission and... prejudices the implementation of the Treaty". But unlike Collins, Cosgrave undertook not to take unofficial action. Cosgrave guaranteed that the Free State army would not interfere in the North. At last the British leaders began to feel that the Treaty would be fulfilled and that Southern Ireland would no longer be a burden to them.

WINSTON IS HOPEFUL OF THE IRISH

Some days later Winston, writing to an ex-lady friend, Pamela Lytton, said: "Ireland is going to save itself. No one else is going to. They are a proud and gifted race and they are up against the grimmest facts...It was interesting to see how when their Parliament met on Saturday, there was no oratory or enthusiasm. Responsibility is a wonderful agent when thrust upon competent heads".

At this time domestic events of major importance to Winston were occurring. His wife was due to give birth to their last child, a girl, Mary. This happened in the early hours of the morning of 15 September. Later that same day the final act in the purchase of Chartwell took place.

As Winston had indicated the Provisional Government had a long and bloody road to travel, as the Republicans vowed to keep up the armed struggle. The Government introduced military courts with the power to hand down summary justice, including death. An order was published on 10 October to take effect five days later. An amnesty would be in effect in the meantime for those who surrendered their arms and ended hostilities. In mid October Cosgrave's own uncle and O'Higgins' father were killed by the I.R.A. This only served to heighten the bitterness between both sides, which suited Churchill, who sent this message to Cosgrave: "It is indeed a hard service that is now exacted from those who are building the Irish State and Nation and defending its authority and freedom". Alfed Cope wrote to Churchill's secretary from Dublin on 14 October: "You may care to convey the following to Mr. Churchill. The leaders here, including the army leaders, have absolute confidence in Mr. Churchill. They have on several occasions expressed to me their appreciation of the manner in which he and the other British signatories are keeping their side of the bargain".

WINSTON'S ACTIONS ENDS COALITION GOVERNMENT

As Winston led a busy and fruitful domestic life throughout the negotiations on Ireland, so too did he have to concern himself with other matters of major international import, as Secretary of State for the Colonies. One of these concerned Turkey and specifically the town of Chanak on the eastern shore of the Dardenelles. Lloyd George had pursued an anti-Turk and a pro-Greek policy in latter years. Churchill did not agree with this. In mid 1922, the Turkish nationalist leader, Mustapha Kemal, pushed the Greeks to the edge of the Smyrna peninsula. Then he began to move northward to threathen the neutral zone of the Dardenelles. The Turks reached the town of Chanak where the British had a small garrison. The Cabinet, with Winston in best jingoistic form, decided to resist any Turkish action to occupy the Gallipoli Peninsula. On 15 September the Government sought Dominion support for their proposed action. But before the Dominions actually received the Government request, Winston issued a public communique on the matter. This upset the Dominions greatly as well as the French and Italian governments, which were also to be involved as allies. As we have seen, Winston did have a lot of domestic and business matters on his mind that particular day. His precipitious action isolated Britain in the Chanak affair. But the Cabinet decided to push ahead. On 29 September, it gave instructions to their forces to attack the Turks unless they withdrew. The British General on the spot ignored the order and sought to solve the matter by negotiation in a peaceful manner.

In Britain some Conservatives had been dismayed at this drift to another war. This found public display, when the then retired, Bonar Law, sent a letter to the Times on 7 October 1922, expressing his condemnation of the Government. He made it clear that much of the Conservative Party opposed the action of the Coalition Government in provoking a war, which would be totally unnecessary. He wrote: "We cannot act alone, as the policeman of the world". He had Churchill in mind in particular as one who would have been happy to plunge the country into an unnecessary war. Winston admitted this was indeed so, as he told Sir Maurice Hankey on 17 October.

An Independent Conservative decided to challenge the Government as an anti-Coalition candidate, at a by election on 18 October. Conservative Ministers held a caucus to discuss their position in government and at a future General Election. Most felt they should remain loyal to the Government and to the Liberals. But the Independent Conservative candidate, to everyones great surprise, won the by election. Nothing concentrates the minds of members of Parliament more, than the danger of losing their seats. That same day a meeting took place of 274 Conservative members at the Carlton Club to discuss their strategy. The motion before the meeting read: "That this meeting of Conservative Members of the House of Commons declares its opinion that the Conservative Party, whilst willing to cooperate with the Coalition Liberals, should fight the election as an independent party, with its own leader and its own programme". Bonar Law and Stanley Baldwin spoke strongly for the motion which was in effect a vote to abandon Lloyd George, who was awaiting the result anxiously. 187 voted for the motion, with 87 voting for the status quo. The Conservative Ministers had split almost in the middle with their leader, Neville Chamberlain supporting Lloyd George. But the majority did not want to take the risk of allowing Lloyd George the opportunity of ruining the Conservative Party, as he had the Liberal Party. Four days later Lloyd George resigned and the King asked Bonar Law to form a government, which he did, and almost immediately announced a general election.

CHURCHILL LOSES CABINET OFFICE

Winston had been out of circulation for the previous few days, having been taken seriously ill on 16 October, the day before the Carlton Club meeting. He was treated first for gastroenteritis, but two days later he had an emergency appendix operation. In those days this was a serious operation, but he survived well. When he awoke afterwards, he wrote: "I learned that the Lloyd George Government had resigned, and I had lost not only my appendix but my office as Secretary of State for the Dominions and Colonies". Winston wrote a final letter to the Irish leader, W.T. Cosgrave on 25 October saying "No one knows better than I, the unceasing, tormenting struggle which was forced on Mr. Arthur Griffith and General Michael Collins, from the moment when the Treaty between the two nations was signed". Mr. Cosgrave replied with great sensitivity and courage to one who had been succeedingly, foe and friend: "The valedictory message which you have sent me on leaving office touches many cords. Hitherto the exit of a British Cabinet from power, has meant for us in Ireland but another milestone, on the long dark road of alien government imposed on our nation, shadowed with futility in rule on the one hand, and utter bitterness in resistance on the other. But in our day and generation, we have found the turn in the road". The subsequent general election on 15 November saw the demise of the old Liberal Party, with the Lloyd George wing and the Asquith wing, not uniting effectively. The result was Conservatives 345; Labour 142; Asquith Liberals 60; Lloyd George Liberals 57.

Winston had not been able to travel to Dundee for the early days of the election. So Clementine, though still feeding her new baby, went there on 5 November to speak on his behalf. She got a very rowdy reception. The local paper, the Dundee Courier, described her as having her ' unbaptised infant ' with her. She wrote to Winston saying that the local Liberal organisation was in chaos and that the local press was vile. His part in settling the Irish and Boer questions were most popular she told him, but added that he also had the name of being a 'War Monger'. She was very realistic about his reelection prospects, saying she would be heartbroken if he was not reelected.

CHURCHILL LOSES SEAT IN GENERAL ELECTION

Though still recuperating Winston travelled to Dundee four days before voting. He got a very hostile reception from the public. At one meeting the local paper quoted him as saying, "The electors will know how to deal with a party (Socialists) whose only weapon is idiotic clamour", before pandemonium broke out in the hall. As well as the 'war mongerer' tag, Winston also had to contend against the women's vote for the first time. Ever since his tenure as Home Secretary, when the police man-handled suffraggettes in Parliament Square in London, women activists reacted adversely to him. He had tried to equivocate in Parliament saying that he had not ordered any police measures, when he had earlier taken a different line. The son of Emily Pankhurst has said; "My mother believed that Winston Churchill was an ambitious politician, whose behaviour was less than honest". On the day of the election the same Dundee Courier editorialised on Churchill saying: "...in a vile temper. He takes no pain to conceal the fact. Like a disappointed man on the station platform, he kicks out at anybody who happens to be near him. He has sprayed Labour with invective". The final result was a shattering blow for Winston and all who cared for him. Of 151,701 votes cast, Winston got 20,000, a mere 13%. He was roundly defeated and dermoralised. T.E. Laurence (Laurence of Arabia) commented, "What bloody shits the Dundeeans must be?"

SOMETHING FOR OLD IRELAND

Leaving Dundee the day after the election Winston was surrounded by a large crowd of university students at the railway station. Unlike many of the people he had encountered in recent days, these were friendly. They sang songs bringing Churchill's name into the refrains. "One or two Irish in the party were specially demonstrative, and one waxed so enthusiastic that he lost his eye glasses, which were trampled and broken under the feet of the crowd swaying round the carriage door. Heedless of his loss, this enthusiastic Irishman, again and again called for 'Cheers for Churchill], his slogan being, 'Up Churchill', Up Collins. Collins believed in you, we believe in you'. Mrs Churchill who was smiling cheerily, then shook hands all round, and there were further cries of 'Cheers for Mrs Churchill'.

'Say a few words Mr. Churchill', was an appeal which after a few moments hesitation, he did not let pass unheeded. Leaning out of the compartment window, Mr. Churchill said he expressed from the very bottom of his heart, his appreciation of those boys coming down. They were very kind. He then referred to the right of the people to reject him in a democratic though painful form... 'Nothing has given me greater pleasure than the fact that during the last year that I have represented Dundee, I have been able to do something for old Ireland'.

This reference to Ireland sent the Irish students of the party into further ecstacies and renewed cries of 'good old Churchill' resounded up and down the station".

Winston then aged forty eight years and feeling depressed, after such an unexpected humiliation, decided to leave England for a four month period. He rented a villa on the Mediterranean, near Cannes, where he wrote, painted, gambled, and recovered from the rigors of political life.

TWO ENGLISHMEN DIFFER

The civil war in Ireland got more violent with the Military Courts sentencing to death, those found carrying arms. One such person was Erskine Childers. He had been arrested on 10 November. In the Times of 13 November, Churchill had described Childers as, "the mischief-making murderous renegade". Though English born and a veteran of the Great War, Childers was an avowed Irish republican. This Churchill could not forgive, though Childers had been part of the Irish delegation at the Treaty negotiations. Before his execution, Childers wrote,: "I feel what Churchill said about my ' hatred ' and 'malice' against England...I die loving England and praying that she may change completely and finally towards Ireland". DeValera said after the execution: "If it is not the people's will that a faithful and loyal servant should be sacrificed to any of Churchills hate, then within an hour, you will rise up and fling from the positions they have usurped and dishonoured, those who would dare so to blacken forever the fair name of this nation". In all seventy seven executions took place. The most notorious of these executions, was of four leaders of the I.R.A. who had taken over the Four Courts. They had been in jail for some time when a Government member of the Dail was shot dead. The Government ordered their immediate execution as a reprisal to show the I.R.A. that they intended to prevail. This drastic action had the desired effect and the civil war gradually petered out.

The Irish Free State became a legal entity on 6 December 1922 with a new Constitution. In his book, "The Last Lion", William Manchester, with a great amount of justification, calls Winston Churchill the founder of Ireland

CHAPTER 13

THE ILLUSORY BOUNDARY COMMISSION

Bonar Law resigned as Prime Minister in May 1923 when he discovered that he had cancer. Stanley Baldwin succeeded him. A General Election soon followed on the thorny issue of Trade Protection. The election results were, Conservatives 258, Labour 191, Asquithian and Lloyd George Liberals 158. The Liberals, who were pro-Free Trade supported Labour, which formed a minority government with Ramsay MacDonald becoming Prime Minister. Winston had stood as a Liberal Free Trader at West Leicester, where he spoke violently against Labour. He was again defeated.

One of Winston's most energetic workers in the campaign was a renegade Irishman named Brendan Bracken. Bracken was born in County Tipperary and educated by the Jesuits at Mungret College in Limerick. His father had been a founder member of the nationalistic Gaelic Athletic Association, but his son rejected his country and his Catholic religion, seeking to become accepted as an upperclass Englishman. "How an unknown and very couth youngster of 22 was able to impose himself on one of the greatest men in England as a boon companion, is a question that admits of no easy answer". Bracken was a journalist and publisher, who proved very successful at his job and got to know Churchill in the beginning through this route, when he was recommended to Churchill by a fellow journalist. Winston was aghast at the arrival of a

Labour Government, calling it a national misfortune. He wrote to the Times suggesting the King might refuse to ' enthrone the Labour Government on the recommendation of Parliament '. When the Liberals supported Labour, he quickly turned towards supporting the Conservatives again. He began to say "Anyone can rat, but it takes talent to re-rat".

In March 1924 Winston stood as an Independent and Anti-Socialist candidate, in a by election in Westminister, with a lot of Conservative party support. But despite this he was defeated by an official Conservative, though by a margin of only forty three votes. The future Labour peer, Fenner Brockway was third. Brendan Bracken was again to the fore in this campaign. Without consulting Winston's wife, he had the Churchill children driven round the constituency in a cart sporting a placard reading "Vote for my Daddy". Bracken, trying to hide his background, was vague about where he came from, and soon a rumour spread that he was in fact Winston's illegitimate son from South Africa. Bracken, like Birkenhead before him and Beaverbrooke later, were not highly thought of by Clementine. But they remained intimates of Churchills'.

CHAMBERLAIN RECOMMENDS CHURCHILL FOR CABINET

In the General election of 1924, Winston eventually regained a Parliamentary seat. He stood as a Constitutionalist at Epping, where he was supported by the leader of the Conservative Party, Stanley Baldwin. The latter became Prime Minister on Labours' defeat. Baldwin made radical changes in the new Conservative Government so as to exert his authority. He discussed the formation of the Cabinet with the King and told him that he intended to bring Churchill in: "it was better to give him office now rather than run the chance of his having a grievance and being disgruntled at being omitted". Winston himself expected some office. The Cabinet Secretary, Tom Jones, told Baldwin that he too felt Winston should be included. Baldwin consulted with Neville Chamberlain who rejected the Treasury for Health. They then discussed the furore which was bound to arise on the inclusion of Churchill and Chamberlain suggested sending Winston to the Treasury. This is what Baldwin did immediately afterwards, telling Winston he was offering him the Chancellorship. Winston thought it was the Chancellorship of the Duchy of Lancaster, the lowest post in Cabinet, he was being offered once again. But then Winston realised almost in disbelief, that it was the Chancellorship of the Exchequer that was on offer. He became emotional and almost overcome with gratitude, stammering to Baldwin that even his friend Lloyd George, had never done so much for him. Once more shades of his father reappeared as Randolph had held that high office before resignation. Winston told Baldwin that he still had his father's robes as Chancellor, and that he would be proud to serve in that splendid office. He rushed down to Chartwell to give the news to Clementine. He told her that the salary was £5,000 and they would have a house in London. They would be free to sell their London home.

By a strange twist of fate, the final act of the Treaty with Ireland was about to unfold, and from his new Office, Winston would be called upon by the Prime Minister to play an important role. A crucial element in the Treaty for Collins and Griffith, was that of the probability, that if and when the North opted out of the terms of the agreement, a Boundary Commission would cede large parcels of the North to the South. In September of 1924 Winston spoke of fixing a border in Ireland, "On the one side will be Catholics, tending more and more towards Republicanism: on the other, Protestants, holding firmly to the British Empire and the Union Jack...No result could be more disastrous to Irish National aspirations". He suggested forgetting the Boundary Commission and hope for "an Ireland free, united, the friend of Britain and a proud cofounder and coheritor of its world-wide Commonwealth". As Chancellor Winston had decided to back a substantial sum for continued heavy policing of the North saying Craig," had not been able to reduce his constabulary...owing to the setting up of the Boundary Commission. It seemed to me always that it should be a point of honour with the British Parliament to sustain and support the Ulster Government, during the early difficult years under the new conditions". During the previous five years the cost of maintaining the Special Constabularies in the North had been £7.5 millions of which the British government contributed £6.75 millions.

THE LETTER OF THE TREATY

..Article 12 of the Treaty had said ' A Commission consisting of three persons, one to be appointed by the Government of Northern Ireland, and one to be appointed by the government of the Irish Free State, and one who shall be Chairman, to be appointed by the British government, shall determine in accordance with the wishes of the inhabitants, so far as may be compatible with economic and geographic conditions, the boundaries between Northern Ireland and the rest of Ireland".

In 1925 the Irish Free State Government felt that it finally had to face up to the implications of Article 12, and put it behind them. Sir James Craig had always said that he would not yield one inch of the North. Northern Nationalists had been somewhat mollified by the expectation that justice would yet be done for their incarceration in a State to which they owed no allegiance and which offered them only discrimination. DeValera and the republicans of the South urged that action be taken to recover the lost territories. Though it can be argued that Sinn Fein, by its abstentionist policy in the Dail had abandoned the Northern Nationalists. The British Government originally, certainly saw some Northern territory being handed to the South by a Boundary Commission, but at this stage it depended on precisely what Article 12 said and how it was interpreted. The Chairman of the Boundary Commission would have the final say. Craig refused to even appoint a person to the Commission, the British Government having to do so. The Chairman was a South African judge who had been educated at Oxford, by name Feetham. The Free State appointed Eoin MacNeill, a cabinet minister, a Northerner who had tried to countermand the 1916 Rising. The Commission deliberated in great secrecy with the respective Governments not being privy to the results.

On 7 November the Conservative Morning Post published details of what it claimed authoritatively were the final and agreed recommendations of the Commission. These would see the Free State giving up East Donegal and getting South Armagh, a much larger and more highly populated enclave. This caused a crisis in the South and Eoin MacNeill resigned from the Commission as hostility to such an agreed report mounted. The report in the newspaper was not confirmed or denied. It suited both the British Government and the North, though both of these knew the predicament in which it would place Cosgrave's Government. Fears grew of a Republican take-over in the South. An emergency meeting of the three Governments was agreed for Chequers later in the month.

It was generally agreed that two options were before them. The existing boundaries could be left, with some concessions to the South to make that palatable, or else the reported conclusions of the Commission could be accepted. Kevin O'Higgins spoke bitterly to Craig of the difficulties of the nationalists within the North. He told British ministers who recalled the policies of the old Irish Parliamentary Party at Westminister, "we are not the heirs of Redmond and Dillon". When O'Higgins discovered that even the nationalist town of Newry might have to remain within the North, it was felt wiser not to consider in detail the reported findings of the Commission. Craig retorted that the South had put too much store on the Boundary Commission, which he said was merely a device to ease acceptance of the Treaty. It was clear that whatever Lloyd George had intended the Boundary Commission to do, it now had fallen to Judge Feetham to so decide. He had the job of interpreting the Article and did so in a strict and legalistic way which meant that no major changes were ever on the cards, merely a fine tuning of the existing border, without any reference to those living there.

CHEQUERS STALEMATE ENDED BY CHURCHILL

The atmosphere at Chequers over that weekend meeting was very tense, with Mrs Baldwin trying to be friendly to all sides. She got all the Irish participants to sign her visitors book. Occasionally she got signs from her husband that all was going well, though with difficulty. Eventually the Free State leaders decided that their best option probably, was to accept the existing border and negotiate other measures which would help sell the deal in the South. This would have to be done at other meetings in London during the following week. As all the Irish travelled together back to London, their car punctured and as they waited by the roadside they engaged in friendly banter. Craig told his fellow passengers that now that the Commission report was to be buried, he would "help you get all I can to get as much as you can out of these fellows". In London Craig told Baldwin that from his conversations with O'Higgins, that if Article 5 of the Treaty could be eased for the Irish, the Boundary Report could be shelved and the existing borders maintained.

It was at this juncture that Baldwin decided that he should hand the negotiations over to Churchill's Chairmanship, as Article 5 concerned itself exclusively with finance. The Article said that Ireland should assume liability for the service of the public debt and payment of war pensions "in such proportions as may be fair and equitable". The Irish wanted this liability waived. But Baldwin felt that this was not possible as huge sums of money were involved to the Exchequer. Another series of tripartite meetings then took place over a few days with Churchill, Birkenhead and Lord Salisbury on the British side. What was remarkable about these was the bi-partisanship of the two Irish Governments. As Birkenhead wrote "They both developed a friendly and competitive enthusiasm in the task of plundering us". It was fortuitous that it was Churchill who was in charge of these negotiations, for he above all British politicians, knew that financial measures could not be allowed wreck what had been achieved in Ireland. In the end, the Irish Free State accepted a bill of £8 millions in continuing land annuities, and had a bill of £155 millions in public debt, waived. Craig told Churchill, "You have done the right thing in a big way". Craig himself would loose financially as the British Government would no longer subsidise the cost of keeping his Special constabularies in existence. But he got the promise of secure borders which was his main interest..Kevin O'Higgins remarked, "The best days work I ever did, and the best for Ireland". The Agreement was signed by the three Governments on 3 December 1925.

COSGRAVE THE PRAGMATIST

This Agreement was vilified by the Republicans who used it to deride and decry Cosgrave's Government as having sold out to the British. The Republicans, from their safety of abstentionist politics, further regarded themselves as the only unsullied inheritors of the 1916 Republic. They continued to promise Northern Nationalists that they would be liberated at the earliest opportunity. The ethos of republican non-democratic violence continued to be cultivated as perfectly permissable in the struggle to 'free' Ireland. One factor which helped lessen Northern nationalist outrage was the split which existed between the Catholics of Belfast and the rest of the North. Those Catholics living in Belfast wanted as many of their co-religionists as possible to remain within the North on the premise that that would provide better safety for the Belfast Catholics. A four county North would have been an absolute disaster. Cosgrave and his Government set their face towards a pragmatic and friendly attitude to Britain and the North. He told the Belfast Telegraph on 4 December 1925:

"I firmly believe that we have found the only solution in a very difficult situation to which the representatives of all of the Governments could have subscribed. I believe that the result is a sane and constructive one, and that it will tend to foster cordial relations, a better understanding, and a greater measure of mutual respect and goodwill. It will remove obstacles which have ever been a source of bitter conflict between the peoples of Northern Ireland and the Irish Free State". Of course those most satisfied by this Agreement was the Northern Government. In the following year they showed their gratitude to Churchill. Craig invited Winston and Clementine to Belfast, as welcome guests. Winston was conferred with an honorary degree at Queens University. It was a return visit filled with irony. Winston addressed the faithful Unionists at the Ulster Hall, where earlier they had denied him the right to speak, and he had to repair to Catholic West Belfast. But now he was firmly on their side and spoke in terms they appreciated, that of the 'Ulster People' being synonymous with the 'Protestant People'. He said:

"I have declared again and again that neither by threats, violence, or intrigue, nor yet by unfair economic pressure shall the people of Ulster be compelled, against their wish, to sever ties which bind them to the United Kingdom, or be forced, unless by their choice, to join another system of Government".

CHAPTER 14

CHURCHILL'S FEARS CONFIRMED

A Labour Government was returned to power in 1929. This election saw Brendan Bracken become a Conservative member of Parliament for North Paddington. He was at this time a wealthy publisher. He and Winston had an undefined disagreement for the previous few years, but this was gradually repaired, as Bracken took the opportunity of defending the ex-Chancellor, when he came under criticism for his handling of that portfolio in the Commons. Great economic difficulties were affecting Britain, in common with many other countries. In 1931 a National Government was formed by the Labour Leader, Ramsay MacDonald and Stanley Baldwin. When news of this development came, Winston and Bracken were on a yachting holiday at Biarritz. Together they rushed back to London, but to their disappointment, Winston was not invited to join the new Government. Though he continued to be a regular attender at Parliament, sitting on the backbenches, these years 1929-1939 have been referred to as Churchill's 'wilderness years'. Nevertheless he spoke on all matters concerning Ireland, especially when his arch 'villain', DeValera came to power in 1932. He also spoke with great forboding of the coming conflict in Europe, though few listened to him on either issue.

One of his great themes during these years was the breakup of the Empire. He had resigned from Baldwin's shadow cabinet on the issue of giving Dominion Status to India. He dismissed the Indian claim as "absurd and dangerous pretensions". When the Statute of Westminster, which sought to establish the effective independence of the Dominions, was being debated, he tried to have the Irish Free State omitted, "as this Bill confers upon the Irish Free State full legal power to abolish the Irish Treaty... It would be open to the Dail... to repudiate the Oath of Allegiance... they could repudiate the right of the Imperial Government to utilize, for instance, the harbour facilities at Berehaven and Queenstown". He sought to introduce an amendment to the Bill: "Nothing in this Act shall be deemed to authorise the Legislature of the Irish Free State to repeal, amend, or alter the Irish Free State Agreement Act 1922, or so much of the Government of Ireland Act 1920, as continues to be in force in Northern Ireland".

DOMINION STATUS

W.T. Cosgrave wrote to Ramsay MacDonald about these efforts. "He, 'trusted that it was quite unnecessary for him to say that 'the Statute of Westminster in its present form' represented an agreement between all the Governments of the Commonwealth, an agreement which had been considered at great length by the Irish representatives at the Imperial Conference and endorsed, as it stood, by Dail and Senate.'. 'Any amendment' he concluded 'of the nature now suggested would be a departure from the terms of the Imperial Conference Report and would be wholly unacceptable to us... You will agree that this is a time when the interests of the peoples of the commonwealth as a whole, must be put before the prejudices of the small reactionary elements in these islands'. Churchill's clear intention was to deprive the Irish Free State of the same Dominion Status as the rest of the

Commonwealth. In this he was not being anti- Southern Irish. He was merely being consistent with his vision of all Ireland as being an integral part of the United Kingdom. He hoped and believed that an all-Ireland Parliament would eventually see the wisdom of this. The further the Free State went from the Imperial Parliament, the less likelihood he knew that this would happen. But his power with Parliament was very low. Baldwin rejected any restrictive clause as it 'would offend not only the Irish Free State, not only Irishmen all over the world, but other Dominions as well. The Statute of Westminster has to be an act of faith, or it was nothing'. The Act became law on 11 December 1931. It included the Governments of the United Kingdom, Canada, Australia, New Zealand, South Africa, Irish Free State and Newfoundland. Each was to be completely self governing, but united by allegiances to the Monarchy, the succession to which, each Dominion would have a say.

This major new development meant that those who had signed the Irish Treaty as a stepping stone to eventual Irish independence, were proved correct. Desmond Fitzgerald wrote:

"Knowing the history of these last years, as I do, I am amazed at the way we have changed the situation... the Free State is (or will be in a couple of years - without even a vestige of any form even to mar it) just a constitutional Monarchy - with only that to make the difference between it and an Irish Republic...In these matters of independence and sovereignty there is no whittle of difference...By accepting the Treaty we certainly are getting all that the most fervid supporters were claiming for it - and more".

THE REPUBLICAN DEVALERA TAKEOVER

By the end of 1931 Winston's worst nightmares were in danger of coming true. The strong possibility that the person he had endeavoured to keep away from Government in the Free State, might win a General Election and take over. DeValera, though splitting from the diehards of Sinn Fein and the I.R.A., had for a time still abstained from taking his seat in the Dail. He refused to take the Oath of Allegiance to the King, which was mandatory. But the only way to political power was through the Dail and DeValera's new party, Fianna Fail, soon buried their principle and took their seats. They were aided in this by arguing that if they had been in the Dail, they could have saved the 'sell-out' of the Boundary Commission fiasco. The civil war was truly over, though its political overtones would linger for generations. Churchill feared that if DeValera came to power he would undo all the good work that had been done with the Irish leaders over the previous ten years. DeValera did come to power in 1932, on a policy of abolishing the Oath of Allegiance to the King and ceasing the payment of the land annuities to Britain.

Churchill wrote of DeValera's victory in a bellicose fashion warning him off any designs on Ulster and telling the people of the South, how they would suffer for DeValera's foolish policies which:

"represents Irish hatred of England... Mr DeValera is unperturbed, careless of the material deprivations which his people are bound to endure; he upholds the ideal of a self-contained Irish Free State... (The British Government retaliated on the land annuities by imposing duties on Ireland's exports to the U.K. This came to be called the Economic War and caused much damage to Ireland)... and here while it is necessary that while they are masters of their own fortunes, they will not be allowed to drag down Ulster into the ditch with them. As long as Ulster wishes to remain an integral part of the U.K., it is a matter of national honour to make sure that they are able to do so. England will defend Ulster, as if it were Kent or Lancashire. We could no more allow hostile hands to be laid upon the the liberties of the Protestants of the North...As long as Ulstermen wish to abide with us, we must abide with them, and give of our power and strength all that is necessary for their safety and due welfare: but let Ulstermen be of good cheer. Until they wish to abandon the British Empire, the British Empire will never abandon them".

OATH OF ALLEGIANCE REPUDIATED

DeValera soon began to dismantle the remaining ties between Britain and the Free State. This gave rise to constitutional controversy and called into question whether the terms of the Treaty or the Statute of Westminster governed relations between the two countries. Churchill could only rise in the Commons and make speeches to the effect that what he had forecast was happening. W.T.Cosgrave too, was not entirely happy with what DeValera was doing. When the proposal to abolish the Oath of Allegiance was introduced in the Dail Cosgrave said: "This Bill...appears to be one of the greatest pieces of political chicanery in history...We have regarded the relations between this country and Great Britain as being based on the Treaty". But DeValera rested his case on the Statute of Westminster and continued dismantling the links. Later Churchill spoke in the Commons of the "dismal catalogue of repudiations" which saw the abolition of the Office of the Governor General, the Irish Senate and the right of appeal to the Privy Council. Winston foresaw that these measures would spread among the other Dominions. A slight hope arose for him that the British government might take a 'stronger line', when Baldwin took over as Prime Minister from MacDonald within the National Government. But worse was to come, despite Winston's efforts.

CONSTITUTIONAL CRISIS

The King of England, Edward VIII, had fallen in love with an American divorcee named Wallis Simpson. He intended to marry her. This introduced a constitutional crisis in Britain and conflict occurred between the King and Baldwin's Government. Winston was a personal friend of Edward's and sought to speak on his behalf in the Commons, only to be shouted down furiously and called a 'twister'. The King decided that he would bow to Government pressure and abdicate so as to marry Mrs Simpson. Lord Birkenhead said to Winston that there was no point going further, "as our cock won't fight". Under the Statute of Westminster all the Dominions had a direct interest and say in the succession to the Throne. All of these immediately agreed to the accession of George VI, except for Ireland. DeValera took the opportunity to eliminate the reference to the King and the Governor General from the Free State Constitution. The King was retained for the purposes of External Association only. An External Relation Act was introduced which said: "... with the following nations, that is to say, Australia, Canada, Great Britain, New Zealand, and South Africa and as long as the King, recognised by these nations as the symbol of their cooperation continues to act on behalf of each of these nations (on the advice of the several governments thereof), for the purposes of the appointment of diplomatic and consular representatives and the conclusion of international agreements, the King so recognised, may, and is hereby authorised to, act on behalf of Saorstat Eireann for the like purposes as and when advised by the Executive Council, so to do". When DeValera introduced a new

Constitution the next year, the British Government said it caused no change in Ireland's position within the Commonwealth.

CHAMBERLAIN THE STATESMAN?

The economic war between Britain and Ireland continued, much to the discomfort of the latter. DeValera was under great pressure to end it. In 1938 he travelled to Britain to meet the Conservative Prime Minister, Neville Chamberlain. They discussed the economic war, partition and the Treaty ports, which Britain still controlled. This element of the Treaty had been one of the most important features of the agreement for Churchill. Now to his consternation, Chamberlain was proposing to hand them over to such a man as DeValera. Winston described it as "an improvident example of appeasement... You are casting away real and important means of security and survival for vain shadows and for ease. Queenstown and Berehaven shelter the flotillas which keep clear the approaches to the Bristol and English Channels, and Lough Swilly is the base from which the access to the Mersey and the Clyde is covered... These are essential bases from which the whole operation of hunting submarines and protecting incoming convoys is conducted". Winston was of course talking about the forthcoming war with Germany. Though in opposition and not even in the shadow Cabinet, he was being kept in touch with military and foreign policy matters by a secret source with the civil service. His information was first class and better than most of the Ministers in the Government. He continued his speech, "In 1922 the Irish Delegates made no difficulty about this... Now we are to give them up, unconditionally, to an Irish Government led by men - I do not want to use harsh words - whose rise to power has been proportionate to the animosity with which they have acted against this country, no doubt in pursuance of their own patriotic impulses, and whose present position in power is based upon the violation of solemn Treaty engagements...The first steps which...an enemy might take would be to offer complete immunity...to Southern Ireland if she would remain neutral". And here Churchill, once again showed how he refused to accept the status of the Free State, as he continued:

"..Southern Ireland is not a Dominion: it has never accepted that position...Southern Ireland... becomes a State which is an undefined and unclassified anomaly... Irish underworld... a whole organisation of secret men, bound together on the old principle that England's danger is Ireland's opportunity". He reminded the members to recall what happened in Ireland during the Great War. One of the few Members who supported Winston in these views was the renegade Irishman, Brendan Bracken.

As the War loomed closer, Winston spoke in his constituency and recalled his unheeded advice to Chamberlain on the Irish ports: "I warned him with my defective judgement that if we got into great danger, Mr. DeValera would demand the surrender of Ulster as the price for any friendship or aid. This fell out exactly. For Mr. DeValera has recently declared that he cannot give us any help or friendship while any British troops remain to guard the Protestants of Ulster". DeValera supported Chamberlain's own appeasement policy and was among the keenest supporters of the Munich Agreement with Hitler. So too were practically all the other Dominions. DeValera had told British Ministers that he had his own Sudetan in Northern Ireland, and that he had even thought sometimes of the possibility of going over the boundary and pegging out the territory which was occupied by a population predominantly in sympathy with Eire and leaving Northern Ireland to deal with the situation. Chamberlain had told DeValera that concessions to him on Partition were not possible given British public opinion. He also told him that there would be no objection to an anti-Partition campaign in Britain. The American Minister in Dublin, David Gray, sounded out the various parties to Partition, on behalf of President Roosevelt, who was always conscious of the Irish-American lobby in the U.S.A. One of the latter, Joseph Kennedy, was then American Ambassador in London. There, Churchill, when consulted, said these matters were "all up to Ulster". He would go along with any agreement which the two Irish Governments came to, as long as that was not against Britain's interests.

CHAPTER 15

SECOND WORLD WAR

Despite the triumphant return of Chamberlain from Munich, saying that he had brought 'peace with honour', Churchill thought very differently and said so. Exposing himself to great unpopularity in the Commons, he declared the Agreement,' a total and unmitigated defeat... all is over. Silent, mounful, abandoned, broken, Czechoslovakia recedes into the darkness'. This speech almost lead to his own constituency disowning him, where the vote split three to two in his favour. But Winston was not alone in his views. Clement Attlee called the Munich Agreement 'a victory for brute force... one of the greatest diplomatic defeats that this country and France have ever sustained'.

The Government had a motion before the Commons on 18 November 1938 to create a Ministry of Supply. For the first time during these 'wilderness years', Winston voted against his party's government. He was joined by Harold MacMillan and the faithful Brendan Bracken. But they were lone Conservative voices. It was not until March 1939,when Germany occupied Czechoslovakia that most people realised the folly of the Munich Agreement. Churchill had drawn the ire of his party, and even that of Hitler himself, for his attitude. The invasion of Czechoslovakia stunned the world. Chamberlain, who was an honourable man, was devastated. Churchill wrote, 'The blow has been struck...Hitler has broken every tie of good faith with the British and the French who tried so hard to believe in him. A veritable revolution in feeling and opinion has occurred in Britain and reverberates through all the self governing Dominions. Indeed a similar process has taken place spontaneously throughout the whole British Empire'.

As the certainty of a war with Germany grew, so did the campaign that it was essential to have Winston in the Cabinet. This was particularly true of the Press, where the Daily Telegraph, the Manchester Guardian and the Daily Mirror were concerned. In March, Churchill, Duff Cooper and Anthony Eden, got thirty signatures in the Commons supporting a National Government. Chamberlain still hoped that war was not inevitable. But in August 1939, Germany signed an ominous treaty with Russia, protecting her Eastern flank. On 1 September Germany invaded Poland. The next day Winston was invited to become First Lord of the Admiralty. It was twenty five years since he had last held the post. Once more he answered the call to war with relish. Writing of his feelings he said,'As I sit in my place, listening to the speeches, a very strong sense of calm came over me... I felt a security of mind and was conscious of a kind of uplifted detachment from human and personal affairs. The glory of Old England,peace-loving and ill prepared as she was, but instantly fearless at the call of honour, thrilled my being and seemed to lift our fate to those spheres far removed from earthly facts and physical sensations'. One of Churchill's first acts at the Admiralty was to ask Brendan Bracken to become his Parliamentary Private Secretary.

In Ireland DeValera had declared the Irish Free State neutral. He said, " It is not sufficient for us to indicate our attitude. It is necessary to take every step... to avoid giving to any of the belligerents any due cause of complaint. When you have powerful States in a war of this sort ... the neutral State,if it is a small State, is always open to considerable pressure...We, of all nations, know what force used by a stronger nation against a weaker one means. We know what invasion and partition mean".

Irish neutrality did not please Churchill. By October 1939 he had advised the Cabinet to 'take stock of the weapons of coercion'. He described the Irish approach as 'odious', and said he was 'sick' of them. He queried their neutrality saying "nothing has been defined. Legally I believe they are at war but skulking". All of Churchill's foreboding about the Irish and DeValera were coming true. The IRA too, though still an illegal organisation in the Irish Free State, choose that same year of 1939 to launch a bombing campaign in England.

The loss of the Irish ports appeared of crucial importance to the defence of British shipping bringing in vital supplies. The war of the U boats was being fought off the coast of Ireland. Churchill harboured suspicions that the Germans might be using the Irish ports. He asked, "what does Intelligence say about possibly succouring of U boats by Irish malcontents in the west of Ireland? If they throw bombs in London, why should they not supply fuel to the U boats? Extreme vigilance should be practised". It was clear that Churchill realised that DeValera might not be a totally free agent as he wrote, "Three quarters of the people of Southern Ireland are with us, but the implacable malignant minority can make so much trouble, that DeValera dare not do anything to offend them. All this talk about partition and the bitterness that would be healed by a union of Northern Ireland will amount to nothing. They will not unite at the present time and we cannot in any circumstances see the loyalists of Northern Ireland down". Though Winston realised that he could not make political decisions on behalf of the Government, he intended to have all the possible military possibilities covered. He instructed the First Sea Lord, "If the U boat campaign became more dangerous, we should coerce Southern Ireland both about coast watching and the use of Berehaven".

CHURCHILL AS PRIME MINISTER

The war went very badly in 1940 on the continent. On 8 May Chamberlain sought a vote of confidence in the Commons. He was heavily criticised from his own party. The veteran Tory, Leo Amery, quoting Cromwell's famous words, said to Chamberlain, "Depart, I say, and let us have done with you. In the name of God go". Chamberlain won the vote by 281 to 200. But the Tory rebels refused to promise future support for the government, unless Labour and the Liberals were brought in. Labour refused to serve under Chamberlain who nominated Lord Halifax to succeed him. Labour rejected Halifax and Churchill became the agreed compromise candidate for Prime Minister. Chamberlain remained in the War Cabinet, though Clement Atlee became Deputy Prime Minister. Anthony Eden also joined the Cabinet.

In his famous acceptance speech, Winston told the British people that, "I have nothing to offer but blood, toil, tears and sweat". He had reached the pinnacle of his career, though in somewhat desperate circumstances. Parliament, reading the times, realised that dire remedies were necessary if the country was to survive. It put its faith in the arch outsider, in the short-term at least, until it saw how the situation developed. Winston was well aware of that reality. As Prime Minister, Churchill wrote to DeValera, "I look forward with confidence to continued friendship between our two countries and you may rely upon me to do my utmost to ensure this". DeValera replied, "I thank you for your message, which is cordially reciprocated". On 23 May DeValera told Churchill that if Germany attacked Ireland, she would resist and call in British help, but there was no question of inviting in British troops before an actual German descent.

Churchill nominated Brendan Bracken to be a member of the Privy Council. When the King felt 'surprised and not a little disturbed' Winston wrote to the Royal Secretary on 2 June 1940, "Mr. Bracken is a member of Parliament of distinguished standing and exceptionable ability. He has sometimes been almost my sole supporter in the years when I have been striving to get this country properly defended, especially from the air. He has suffered, as I have done, every form of official hostility. Had he joined the ranks of the time-servers and careerists who were assuring the public that our air force was larger than that of Germany, I have no doubt, that he would long ago have attained high office". Bracken was duly appointed to the Privy Council. Later in July 1941 Churchill appointed him Minister for Information.

Belgium and Holland fell to the Germans and in June France too collapsed.

AN OFFER OF IRISH UNITY?

The possibility of a German invasion of Ireland exercised the mind of the British Government during 1940. Ernest Bevin, a Labour member, commissioned a study from Lionel Curtis, a central character in the 1921 Treaty negotiations. Curtis reported to the Cabinet in mid June. The outcome of this was a 'Joint Executive Authority for the defence of Ireland for the duration of the war, consisting of members of the Cabinets of

Southern and Northern Ireland, with DeValera as Chairman'. Churchill's response was that he had no objection to Ulster being persuaded, but not coerced. "The key to this is DeValera showing some loyalty to Crown and Empire", Winston said. Chamberlain drafted a British proposal for DeValera. He showed the memo to Churchill who approved it and brought it to Cabinet, where it was unanimously approved. Malcolm MacDonald was sent to Dublin the next day. The memo offered:

1. A British declaration accepting the principle of a United Ireland.

2. The immediate establishment of a North-South body to 'work out the constitutional and other practical details of the union of Ireland'.

3. The immediate establishment of a North-South Defence Council.

4. The South to join the Allies 'forthwith' and to invite British military, naval, and air support to help defend the South against invasion.

5. The South to intern all German and Italian aliens and to suppress the IRA.

6. The British to supply immediate arms supplies to the South. If the Irish agreed, the British would 'at once seek to obtain the assent thereto of the Government of Northern Ireland'.

On 26 June, when James Craig first got a copy of the proposals, he wrote to Chamberlain, "I am profoundly shocked and disgusted by your letter making suggestions so far reaching, behind my back and without preconsultation. To such treachery to loyal Ulster, I will never be a party". Though the offer to the South was even improved upon, DeValera rejected "the purely tentative plan" on 4 July. He knew well that any government of which Churchill was Prime Minister, would never coerce Ulster, unless it was in the clear interest of England itself. James Craig the Northern Ireland Prime Minister, travelled to London, where he had a 'very satisfactory chat' with Churchill, which ended all talk of a United Ireland. Speaking in the Dail in April 1950 of this offer, DeValera said, "We cannot believe you. We believed that if we were foolish enough to accept that invitation...we would be cheated in the end". In 1994 when the DeValera Papers were still being gradually made public, a 1965 letter from Malcolm MacDonald to the then President DeValera, spoke of this episode. MacDonald, who admired DeValera greatly, spoke of his June 1940 visit to DeValera at the behest of Churchill, "to discuss a certain war-time proposal with you... I always believed that your decision was absolutely the right one - although Churchill did not agree with that when I reported to him".

In 1940 as the war was going so badly for the Allies, it was widely believed in Ireland that Germany would be victorious, and that a united Ireland might come out of that. There was also a possibility that the Germans might invade the North of Ireland, where British troops were stationed and whose ports were being used by the British navy. But the Germans were careful not to do anything which might impinge on Irish neutrality. German standing orders were, "Any active interference in Irish internal conflicts... should be avoided. Submarines should avoid Irish territorial waters".

The USA occupied Greenland while Britain occupied Iceland, to prevent any German occupation. Britain offered some military assistance to Ireland, which was accepted. In fact despite so much rhetoric, then and later, Ireland's neutrality was of a very friendly variety towards Britain. She provided Britain with much secret help right throughout the war in a variety of areas. A secret memorandum from the Irish

Department of External Affairs, dated May 1941, details some thirteen such areas. They included, information on transport and military facilities in Ireland, free air space for British planes, broadcasting facilities, collection of and passing on of information, a coast watch service, routing of official German and Italian communications through Britain, internment of spies, use of Shannon airport, blacking out of areas at British request. Ireland also provided much food to Britain.

Despite all the secret assistance, great ill feeling persisted, particularly when any incident occurred, where Ireland's neutrality could be blamed. In the summer of 1940, the ship, the Empress of Britain had been sunk off Donegal. In the Commons Churchill spoke bitterly. He said that 'the fact that we cannot use the south and west coasts of Ireland to refuel our flotillas and aircraft, and thus protect the trade by which both Britain and Ireland live, that fact is a most grievous and burdensome one, which should never have been placed on our shoulders, broad though they be". He wrote to President Roosvelt, "We are denied the use of the ports or territory of Eire in which to organise our coastal patrols by air or sea".

DEVALERA RESPONDS TO CHURCHILL'S TAUNTS

DeValera replied to Churchill's tirade in the Dail:

"...I would have refrained from making any comment on it, were it not that it has been followed by an extensive Press campaign in Britain itself, and reached the USA, the purport of the campaign being that we should surrender or lease our ports to Britain for the conduct of the war". DeValera then went on to say that his government wished to have good relations with Britain, but while partition remained this was difficult. He said that the policy of neutrality had been made clear quite early on and would be maintained with both sides. He advised the British Government that for it to enforce conscription in the North, would 'stir up anew the old bitterness and antagonisms between the peoples of these islands...I have tried not to say anything here which would make it more difficult for the British government to give calm consideration and full weight to the representations that I have made".

On Tuesday 3 December 1940, John Coleville, Churchill's Private Secretary, recorded in his diary that at dinner that evening, Churchill 'conspired' with senior officials about the means of bringing pressure to bear on Ireland, refusal to buy her food, to lend her shipping or to pay her the present subsidies. Colville says that these measures seem calculated to bring DeValera to his knees in a very short time. That same month the agreement by which the British allocated shipping space to Ireland, on condition that the latter did not charter neutral shipping, was abrogated by Churchill. At that point Britain had most neutral shipping contracted, leaving the Irish without the possibility of getting in enough vital supplies. DeValera appealed to the American public with the notion that the British were trying to create another Irish famine. Sir John Maffey, the British representative in Ireland, and Churchill, disagreed on the amount of pressure which could carefully be put on the Irish without antagonising the Irish-American lobby. Roosevelt was also conscious of this danger and was annoyed with DeValera for appealing so directly to the American people.

THREAT OF CONSCRIPTION IN NORTH

The application of conscription to the North became a public issue in the summer of 1941. The North's Government said on

21 May that it was "emphatically of the opinion that conscription should be applied to Northern Ireland. It considers that in this matter, a common basis for the whole of the United Kingdom is just...there may be Nationalist opposition to conscription". On that same day, Churchill, speaking in the Commons said that conscription was being considered for the North. DeValera again protested vigorously. Cardinal MacRory, Catholic Primate of All Ireland, said that it would be "an outrage on the national feeling and an aggression on our national rights...an ancient land was partitioned by a foreign power against the vehement protests of its people, and that conscription would now seek to compel those who still writhe under this grievous wrong, to fight on the side of its perpetrators". Churchill reacted angrily to DeValera, losing his temper as he said, "no obstruction should be put in the way of those who wanted to run away". Churchill's proposal was a major crisis for DeValera, as it could open up barely covered sores, which the IRA would benefit enormously from. He wrote a personal letter to Churchill saying, "The imposition of conscription will inevitably undo all the good that has been done and throw the two peoples back into the old unhappy relations. The conscription of the people of one nation by another revolts the human conscience. No fairminded man anywhere, can fail to recognise in it an act of oppression upon a weaker people and it cannot but do damage to Britain herself. The Six Counties have towards the rest of Ireland a status and relationship which no Act of Parliament can change. They are part of Ireland. They have always been part of Ireland, and their people, Catholic and Protestant, are our people. I beg of you, before you enter on a course which can affect so profoundly the relations of our two peoples, to take all these matters into the most earnest consideration".

The Americans and Canadians urged caution on Churchill, recalling the problems conscription for Ireland caused in 1918. On 27 May, Churchill, to his credit and wisdom, announced in the Commons that conscription would not proceed in the North, arguing that it would be "more trouble than it is worth to enforce such a policy". He praised the North's Government for their 'loyal aid and continued constant support'. As many Irishmen from the South as the North fought for the Allies. In late 1940 the Germans had carried out a detailed feasibility study of invading Ireland, but decided against, unless she received an invitation to do so. The Germans tried to destroy the shipping passing to the north of Ireland, but due to British air patrols flying from the North, they failed to do so effectively. Churchill said that Ulster stood as a faithful sentinel. He began to exert economic pressure on the South by withdrawing subsidies for food. He stopped the supply of fertilizers and feeding stuffs as well as military supplies. He argued that juridically Britain never recognised the South as an independent State and she herself had repudiated Dominion status. He was also clear that should the war effort be threatened by the denial of the South's bases, Britain would act in accordance with its own self preservation.

PEARL HARBOUR

Churchill realised that unless the Americans entered the war there would be no victory over Hitler. He therefore sought to convince Roosevelt and the American public that this was their war too. This was no easy task but Winston worked at it assiduously. DeValera, in June 1940, had contemplated allowing American troops to be stationed in Ireland to guarantee Ireland's neutrality. In April 1941 Roosevelt allocated funds to build bases in the North and in Scotland for

American escort ships. On 7 December 1941 the Japanese attacked Pearl Harbour and catapulted the Americans into the war. The day after Pearl Harbour, Churchill wired DeValera,"Now is your chance. Now or never! A nation once again". Roosevelt too sent a message to DeValera, "If freedom and liberty are to be preserved, they must now be defended by the human and material resources of all the free nations. Your freedom too is at stake". DeValera made no reply to Roosevelt. America's entry into the war meant that she was now one of the belligerents, and as such unwelcome in neutral Ireland.

Churchill and Roosevelt agreed in Washington in January 1942, that American troops would be stationed in Northern Ireland. Sir John Maffey, informed DeValera of their arrival on 26 January and begged him not to lodge any objection. The Americans were met with all due pomp by the North's Prime Minister, the Governor-General and American Ambassador to Great Britain. It was the successful culmination of Churchill's plans to thwart DeValera's neutrality and bring American forces into the war. Churchill relished the loyalty of the North for Britain in her hour of need, unlike the ungrateful South. The bond between him and the North became unbreakable. DeValera, rejecting Maffey's entreaties, protested that the American presence in the North was in breach of his jurisdiction. Once more he outlined the injustices of partition, saying that the Irish people had no feeling of hostility towards, and no desire to be brought into conflict with the USA. But he said that the maintenance of partition was as indefensible as aggression against small nations elsewhere, which he noted was the avowed purpose of Britain and America being in the war.

At that stage Churchill decided that the Southern ports were not absolutely essential. He decided to leave the ongoing pressurising of the South to the Americans while he concentrated on continental fronts. He refused to elaborate on this to DeValera, saying that "I think it would be better to let DeValera stew in his own juice for a while".

In retrospect, it can only be of the utmost relief that neither the British nor the Germans invaded Ireland. For either to have done so, would have provided the country with a frightening prospect. A British invasion would have revisited the horrors of the Black and Tan period. A German invasion, with their list of four thousand Irish Jews already compiled, might have led to a most ignominious episode in Irish history. A recent visit to Anne Frank's house in Amsterdam, where I saw a map illustrating those countries which gave Jews refuge from Hitler's insanity, has made me less confident about Irish neutrality.

The war continued to go Hitler's way for several years. There seemed to be little possibility of an Allied victory. One disaster led to another. The Commons became restless, fearing that Winston was not going to fulfil his role of saviour. A vote of censure on him was introduced in the House. This was the one body which brought fear into his mind. It had the capacity to end his career at will. But he survived the vote and soldiered on, looking for the breakthrough which would give heart to the Allies. This only came in October 1942 when General Montgomery defeated Rommel in North Africa at the battle of El Alamein. On 15 November the church bells rung out all over Britain in joy at the victory. The tide had at last begun to turn and there was hope that Hitler could be defeated.

David Gray kept in close touch with DeValera's government. Roosevelt told Gray in December 1942 that it was "a pity that Ireland has lived in a dream world under the rule of a dreamer. If and when we do clean up Germany, I think that Winston Churchill and I can do much for Ireland and its future -and I think that he and I can agree on the method with due consideration of firmness and justice". Gray wrote to Roosevelt on 9 January 1943 saying that DeValera had "dammed little time to go into reverse and get on the band waggon, otherwise, he was assuming the responsibility of blocking a settlement for a generation". But DeValera held fast to his policy of neutrality.

EIRE'S FRIENDLY NEUTRALITY

The fact that this was a most friendly neutrality, despite Churchill's ranting and Gray's strictures, was clear. In June 1943 Gray raised the question of bases in Ireland with the American Joint Chiefs of Staff. He was told such would in fact be a liability. When in September of that same year R. Nicolas Carter, head of the American Office of Strategic Overseas Services, came to Dublin to inquire whether Irish diplomats in Berlin, Rome and Vichy, would collect information for the Allies, he got a positive response. Immediate action, on DeValera's instructions followed. This as T. Ryle Dwyer writes "made a mockery of Ireland's supposed neutrality".

Stalin had sent Molotov to London and Washington as early as May 1942 to demand a second front in Europe in the near future. Roosevelt, after consulting with his Chief of Staff, General George Marshall, promised one for that same year. But Churchill after consulting his own military people had to advise that this was impossible. But he assured Stalin that it would take place in 1943. The Allies did invade Sicily in 1943 but this did not satisfy Stalin who regarded this as peripheral to the main European theatre of war. In 1943 at Teheran, Stalin was assured the major invasion would occur in 1944, as he intimated that he might sue for a separate peace with the Germans, then involved in a life or death struggle in Russia against the Red Army.

When the plan for Overlord, the Allied invasion of Europe, was being drawn up, Churchill was very conscious that because of the presence of enemy diplomats in Dublin, there was a danger that such plans might not remain secret. He approached Roosevelt in March 1944 to "take appropriate steps for the recall of German and Japanese diplomats in Ireland". The next day, Sir John Maffey, made a similar request to DeValera. Both requests were refused. Churchill sought to halt all travel between Britain and all of Ireland from 12 March 1944. In the Commons he said, "No one can reproach us with precipitancy. No nation in the world would have been so patient". The day chosen for the invasion of Europe was 5 June. But weather reports emanating from Belmullet in County Mayo to London, caused it to be postponed by one day.

DeValera maintained his role of public neutrality to the very end of the war. When on 30 April 1945 at 12.30, with Germany crumbling, the American Minister Gray, demanded from DeValera the right to take possession of the German files at the German Legation, he was rebuffed. DeValera informed him that he had to consult the Attorney-General about such a matter. Gray duly reported that even at this late stage, DeValera refused to cooperate with the victorious Allies. DeValera played his neutrality to a more extreme degree later that same day, when after the announcement of Hitler's death in Berlin, he went to the German Legation in Dublin, to offer his sympathy on the death of the Fuhrer. He explained this extraordinary act saying that, "to have failed to call upon the German representative would have been an unpardonable discourtesy to the German nation and to Dr. Hempel himself". In fact Hempel, who was not seen as a Nazi, was deeply embarrassed by DeValera's action. The latter defended himself in a letter to Robert Brennan, Irish Ambassador to the USA, saying that it was of "considerable importance that the formal acts of courtesy paid on such occasions as the death of a head of state, should not have attached to them, any further special significance...I acted correctly and I feel certain wisely".

That shocking political gaffe brought even more odium on DeValera and Ireland from the victorious Allies around the world. It left Ireland isolated in her misunderstood policy of neutrality.

VICTORY DAY

Students from Trinity College hoisted a Union Jack on their College, to celebrate Victory Day in Dublin. This action attracted more nationally minded students from nearby University College, who burned a Union Jack opposite Trinity, on College Green. Among these latter group of students was one Charles J Haughey. Bruce Arnold writes, "In celebration of the ending of the war in Europe, students at Trinity College flew the Union Jack from the flagpole facing College Green. Charles Haughey, with a friend, Seamus Sorahan, who was then a law student, burned another Union Jack on a lamp-post outside the College, an action which led to a minor riot".

At the moment of Churchill's greatest triumph, on Victory Day, he was foolish enough in his victory speech, to attack DeValera personally and draw attention to him before a world wide audience. In it Churchill demonstrated that despite his major involvement in taking Ireland to independence, he still did not understand that such a country has a right to exercise that independence. He said:

"...Owing to the action of Mr. DeValera, so much at variance with the temper and instinct of thousands of southern Irishmen, who hastened to the battlefront to prove their ancient valour, the approaches which the southern ports and airfields could so easily have guarded, were closed by the hostile aircraft and U-boats.

This was indeed a deadly moment in our life, and if it had not been for the loyalty and friendship of Northern Ireland, we should have been forced to come to close quarters with Mr. DeValera, or perish forever from the earth.

However, with a restraint and poise, to which I venture to say history will find few parallels, His Majesty's Government never laid a violent hand upon them, though at times it would have been quite easy and quite natural. We left the DeValera Government to frolic with the Germans and later with the Japanese representatives to their hearts content.

I think of these days and of Lieut.-Comdr. Esmonde, V.C.; Lance-Corporal Keneally, V.C.; Capt. Fegen, V.C., and other Irish heroes that I could scarcely recall, and all the bitterness by Britain for the Irish race dies in my heart. I can only pray that in the years which I shall not see, the shame will be forgotten and the glories will endure, and the peoples of the British Isles will walk together in mutual comprehension and forgiveness...".

DeValera's reply came three days later. In it, DeValera did not reply in kind, but was considerate of Churchill's position in making the speech. But DeValera certainly took the high moral ground of the argument which was unanswerable. He said:

"Certain newspapers have been very persistent in looking for my answer to Mr. Churchill's recent broadcast. I know the kind of answer I am expected to make... I know the reply I would have made a quarter of a century ago... Allowances must be made for Mr. Churchill's statement, however unworthy, in the first flush of his victory... Mr. Churchill makes it clear, that in certain circumstances, he would have violated our neutrality and that he would justify his action by Britain's necessity... if accepted, would mean that Britain's necessity would become a moral code and when this necessity became sufficiently great, other people's rights were not to count... That is precisely why we have the disastrous succession of wars...

Mr. Churchill is justly proud of his nations perseverance against heavy odds. But we in this island are still prouder of our peoples perseverance for freedom through all the centuries... I regret that it is not to this nobler purpose that Mr. Churchill is lending his hand, rather than, by the abuse of a people who have done him no wrong, trying to find in a crisis like the present, excuse for continuing the mutilation of our country... Meanwhile, even as a small partitioned nation, we shall go on and strive to play our part in the world, continue unswirvingly to work for the cause of true freedom and for peace and understanding between all nations". The Irish Ambassador to the USA, Robert Brennan, sought to have this speech of DeValera's, put on the record in Congress, but could not find 'one of our old friends' to do so, 'because the atmosphere created here, because of all that, is still bad', he wrote to DeValera. Thus the reality of Ireland's neutrality did not reach an international audience. Several years later, when Winston was completing the sixth volume of his history of the war, he made a significant alteration to the text of his speech attacking DeValera. The Taoiseach's name was deleted from the insulting personal references and in its place was substituted the more anodyne phrase -the Dublin Government. Malcolm MacDonald explained Churchill's view of Ireland thus: "There were things Winston Churchill did not see clearly and did not understand. These old colonialists thought that those who wanted to be independent wanted to be wild men. He didn't attempt to understand DeValera. Because DeValera wanted to get away from the Empire, Churchill though he should be regarded as an enemy of Britain. This dictated his attitude during the war and for some time afterwards. DeValera would not let Britain use the ports in Britain's hour of greatest crisis. For Churchill therefore, DeValera was an enemy, an enemy, an enemy". Small nations, like large ones, act out of absolute self interest. This meant that any inconsistencies between the Irish Government's official neutral position and its action in aiding the Allies were necessary expedients, rather than evidence of hypocrisy. The same was true of Churchill's attitude to Irish neutrality. He would tolerate it unless it was in Britain's vital interest to trample on it.

Chapter 16

TWO ELDER STATESMAN MEET

DeValera's insistence on his country's neutrality during the war, succeeded in establishing its independence among the nations of the world without any doubt. In this he had the almost total backing of his people. But the neutrality had a very negative affect in several ways. It made the South very inward looking and even parochial. It missed participating in an event of world proportions. In contrast the North sought to participate as fully as possible, as an integral part of the United Kingdom. It took up the slack left by the South's neutrality. This had a profound affect on public and official perception in Britain. This was personified in the person of Winston Churchill, who was then even more certain, that the North had earned its keep as part of the Kingdom. This solidified the partition of Ireland and made a united Ireland even more difficult to attain. This was to become institutionalised before the end of the decade.

In March 1945 the British Coalition Government had resigned. Churchill had been very sceptical about Labour's plans for improving social services and widespread nationalisation. Cabinet Ministers had differed in public on major issues. The Conservatives were sure they would be returned to form a Conservative government. Winston was asked by the King to remain on as Prime Minister until the General Election could be held in the summer. This he did until July, with an entirely Conservative Cabinet. As the election results came in the day after the general election, it soon became obvious that Labour was going to be victorious. Churchill decided that he would resign immediately. He went to see the King and then issued a public statement saying, "The decision of the British people has been recorded in the votes counted today. I have therefore laid down the charge which was placed upon me in darker times. I regret that I have not been permitted to finish the work against Japan". Japan would only surrender later on 14 August.

The result of the election was, Labour 393, Tories 213, Liberals 12, Independents 23. Clement Atlee became Prime Minister with Winston Leader of the Opposition. The man who had led Britain through her darkest hour was turned out of office, at the earliest opportunity, by the electorate. Churchill was distraught with the ingratitude of it all. His family and friends were incredulous that he could be rejected at such a time. But the voters had decided to back Labour and its promise of social service improvements and full employment. Yet when one of his team criticised the people, Winston replied that the people had had a lot to put up with over the last few years. Once more, the democrat within him shone forth in the most bitter of circumstances.

IRON CURTAIN

Churchill was therefore denied the opportunity to play a leading role in the post war reconstruction of Europe, when the Americans introduced the Marshall Plan to revivify the shattered economies of western Europe. But he continued to write and speak. As early as March 1946, at a famous occasion in Fulton Missouri, he first used the phrase 'iron curtain', when he warned the western democracies of the onset of totalitarian Communism. He said: "...From Stettin in the Baltic to Trieste in the Adriatic, an iron curtain has descended across the Continent. Behind that line all the capitals of the ancient states of central and eastern Europe, Warsaw, Berlin, Prague, Vienna, Budapest, Belgrade, Bucharest and Sofia. All these famous cities and the populations around them lie in what I must call the Soviet sphere...".

In September 1946, speaking in Zurich Churchill called for a 'United States of Europe', to thwart the menace of Communism. He warned that time may be short, though at present there was a breathing space, when the canons had stopped firing and the fighting had stopped, though the dangers had not. If the United States of Europe was to happen, action had to be taken immediately. The atomic bomb was still only in the hands of a State and nation which would never use it except in the cause of right and freedom. But he foresaw the day when that awful agent of destruction would be widespread and the possibility of disintegrating the globe itself at hand.

Winston's next few years were spent mainly in writing his massive history of the war, which he was uniquely positioned to do. His role as Leader of the Opposition was very much delegated to his Front Bench colleagues. On 24 May 1946, he was trying to ensure that the government would retain British troops in the Canal Zone in Egypt. He warned that to withdraw them would be like handing over the Irish ports in 1938, which 'nearly brought us to our ruin'. This remark brought laughter from the government benches, to which he replied:

"I have heard all this mocking laughter before in the time of a former government. I remember being once alone in the House, protesting against the cession of the southern Irish ports. I remember the looks of incredulity, the mockery, the derision and laughter I had to encounter on every side, when I said that Mr. DeValera might declare Ireland neutral. We are seeing the same thing happening today, although I am not so much alone as I used to be. I would have hardly believed it possible that such things could happen twice in a lifetime".

During August of that same year George Bernard Shaw wrote to Winston praising him and saying that the strain of American democracy and the independent artistic streak in him, had continually made him misunderstood and feared among the blimps and Philllistines. Churchill responded to Shaw hoping that the Irish question could be settled. He suggested calling the long tragedy, quits.

In November 1947,the Churchills indulged in an after dinner charade at Chartwell, when Winston answered questions the ghost of his father, Randolph, asked about Ireland. Winston told him that the South had got Home Rule, which meant Rome rule. But, he said, the Irish liked this, and the Catholic Church was playing a vital role on behalf of individual freedom. He told his father that the status of Ireland was confused, but that relations between their two countries were good. The Irish were making a successful job of their country.

SEAN MACBRIDE MEETS CHURCHILL

In 1948, DeValera too found himself out of office after sixteen continuous years as Taoiseach. One reason for this was the lack of positive moves on the question of partition. The new Foreign Minister, Sean MacBride was a former Chief of Staff of the IRA, who had recently set up a new republican party called Clann na Poblachta. His aim was to press for a more radical approach to partition. The new government would give the Ulster Unionists 'any reasonable guarantees' in pursuance of a united or federal Ireland. MacBride was a very suave diplomat and a pleasant surprise to the British and Americans, who had feared his accession to power. MacBride played a significant international role at the Organisation for European Economic Development, the Marshall Plan and the Council of Europe. He courted Clement Atlee on the matter of partition. Attlee paid a visit to Ireland in the summer of 1948 which included a holiday in the west partly accompanied by MacBride. Attlee seemed to be sympathetic to the cause of Irish unity, but told MacBride that his hands were tied by the public support within Britain for the North. This was personified by Winston Churchill, Attlee told MacBride, adding that if Churchill could be moved, the Labour Government would feel free to be more adaptable. Shortly after his Irish visit Attlee set up a meeting, over dinner in London, between MacBride, Churchill and himself. MacBride reported on this occasion quoting Churchill as saying to him; "I believe your father and I were both in South Africa in 1900, but on opposite sides...It appears that you and I were both at the Anglo-Irish Conference in 1921, but still on opposite sides...It seems we are fated to be adversaries...So much the better because on this question I have my loyalties. I cannot let down my Unionist friends in Ulster". After this discourse, Churchill said nothing else during the course of the dinner.

WORDS OF PRAISE FOR IRELAND

The new Taoiseach John A Costello, somewhat unexpectedly announced in Ottawa in late 1948 that his Government intended to repeal DeValera's External Relations Act and declare a republic. This would also entail Ireland leaving the British Commonwealth. Attlee's Government was not unduly worried by this declaration of intent. But in the Commons, Churchill bemoaned the drift away from the Empire, saying that countries were then only keeping the link to the Crown for economic reasons. He stressed that the example of Ireland being allowed become a republic must be seen as unique and not setting a precedent. In what was to be his last major statement on the Irish question he said:

"I shall always hope that some day there will be a united Ireland, but at the same time, that Ulster or the Northern counties will never be compelled against their wishes to enter a Dublin Parliament. They should be courted. They should not be raped.

As the Minister responsible for carrying out the Cabinet decisions embodied in the Irish Treaty of 1921, I have watched with contentment and pleasure the orderly, Christian society, with a grace and culture of its own and a flash of sport thrown in, which this quarter of a century has seen built up in Southern Ireland, in spite of many gloomy predictions... In the end we got through without this step (retaking the ports). I rejoice that no new blood was shed between the British and the Irish peoples. I shall never forget - none of us can ever forget - the superb gallantry of the scores of thousands of Southern Irishmen who fought as volunteers in the British army, and of the famous Victoria Crosses which eight of them gained by their outstanding valour. If ever I feel a bitter feeling rising in me, in my heart about the Irish, the hands of heroes like Finnucane seem to stretch out to soothe it away. Moreover since the war, great antagonisms have grown up in this world against Communist tyranny and Soviet aggression. These have made new ties of unity of thought and of sympathy between the Irish and British peoples, and indeed throughout the British Islands, and they deeply stir Irish feelings. The Catholic Church has ranged itself among the defenders and champions of the liberty and dignity of the individual. It seemed to me that the passage of time might lead to the unity of Ireland itself in the only way in which unity can be achieved, namely, by a union of Irish hearts.

There can, of course, be no question of coercing Ulster, but if she were wooed and won of her own free will and consent, I, personally, would regard such an event as a blessing for the whole of the British Empire and also for the civilised world".

The declaration of a republic caused the Northern Ireland Government of Basil Brooke major concern. They appealed to Attlee about the creation of a 'Sudetan Situation'. They saw the new policy as one which would foment disturbances in the North, possibly forcing the Southern Government to send troops northwards to protect the nationally minded people. The Republic was duly declared and left the Commonwealth. Attlee's Government then prepared the Ireland Act 1949 which declared, "that Northern Ireland remains part of His Majesty's dominions and of the United Kingdom and it is hereby affirmed that in no event will Northern Ireland or any part thereof cease to be part of His Majesty's dominions and of the United Kingdom without the consent of the Parliament of Northern Ireland".

This Ireland Act would appear to support Winston's firmly held view, that The Irish Free State had legally remained part of His Majesty's Dominions. Section I of the Act stated, 'that part of Ireland heretofore known as Eire ceased, as from 18 April 1949, to be part of His Majesty's Dominions".

DeValera objected vociferously to this Act saying, "If this is done to our country, I say for myself that feelings will be back to what they were in 1919 to 1921. If these people are to tell us that our country can only be united by setting us an impossible task, we hope another way will be found that will not be impossible. We had hoped for something different than that". The Ireland Act also "declared that, notwithstanding that the Republic of

Ireland is not part of His Majesty's dominions, the Republic of Ireland is not a foreign country for the purposes of any law in force in any part of the United Kingdom". The Act did not make much material difference between the two countries.. But the bonds between the North and Great Britain were further strengthened, so that any movement towards a united Ireland was put further away. Churchill emphasised this as he said, "the declaration of the republic dug a ditch, opened a gulf, between the two parts of Ireland". He and Attlee were in agreement that Ulster could not be coerced into joining the Republic.

That same year of 1949 saw the Republic refuse to join the new post-war North Atlantic Treaty Organisation, mainly due to the continuing of partition. Thus the policy of military neutrality was maintained.

It was in late 1951 that Churchill again became Prime Minister,at the age of seventy seven years. This time he was elected to the office. He offered Brendan Bracken a Cabinet post which was refused on health grounds. In 1952 Bracken became a Peer with the title Viscount Bracken of Christchurch. He never took his seat in the Lords and effectively resigned from politics and concentrated on his publishing business. At that time Eamon DeValera was also back in office as Taoiseach. In June 1953 Winston suffered a serious stroke causing partial paralysis and loss of speech. He made a remarkable recovery.

HISTORIC MEETING

On 11 September 1953, Lord Moran, Churchill's doctor recorded him saying, " then on Wednesday there will be a cabinet meeting and DeValera is lunching with me. I am glad it has been possible to arrange this. He is nearly blind, I am told. They'd give me a great reception if I went over to Dublin". DeValera was still feeling isolated internationally and was just

1953 Historic Meeting at Ten Downing Street between the two Prime Ministers, Churchill and DeValera.

after a visit to General Franco of Spain and Antonio Salazar of Portugal, not two of the most popular European democratic leaders. Churchill's invitation to DeValera was therefore most welcome. Lord Moran wrote of Churchill's reaction to the occasion, "DeValera lunched here. A very agreeable occasion. I like the man".

It was widely reported from London, that on Tuesday 15 September DeValera had attended a lunch in his honour with The British Foreign Secretary, Sir Anthony Eden and Lord Swinton, Secretary for Commonwealth Relations. All the Irish papers noted that Sir Winston Churchill was seeing the Queen at Balmoral that same day. There was no hint whatsoever that a meeting between the Prime Minister and the Taoiseach was imminent. The news of the historic meeting caused great surprise. Some prior knowledge did occur in London as when Mr. DeValera's car, flying the Tricolour, arrived at Number Ten Downing St., it was met by the Press and a crowd of more than one hundred people. These latter "cheered the Irish party lustily, though a Police Inspector protested at this display". Sir Winston came out to greet his guest and together they posed for the photographers.

F.H. Boland, the Irish diplomat, who accompanied DeValera reported that "Churchill met us at the door. He greeted DeValera warmly, took him by the arm and said: 'if you shout I shall be able to hear what you say. Now I will lead the way because I can see a little better' ". This brought a general bout of laughter. The two men talked privately for about twenty five minutes before taking lunch. Frank Aiken, Minister for Finance, who accompanied DeValera, said that the two leaders got on well together, discussing over lunch nothing more volatile than higher mathematics. The equation had been squared for them. DeValera's own note of the occasion said, "I spoke first of a possible unification of the country. To this he replied that they could never put out the people of the Six counties,so long as they wished to remain with them. There were also political factors which no Conservative could ignore".

Churchill must have been perplexed when DeValera informed him that he would not have taken Ireland out of the Commonwealth, as John A Costello had done in 1949. DeValera realised that continuing membership of that organisation would have been in Ireland's interests.

It has become clear with the 1994 release of some of DeValera's papers that he also requested Churchill to release the remains of Sir Roger Casement to his relatives for reburial in

Ireland. Churchill subsequently wrote to DeValera regretting that his government could not comply with this request. Churchill said the law forbade it and there was the need not to reawaken "the bitter memories of old differences". DeValera replied accepting neither excuse. He argued that his legal advisors said the disposal of the body was at the absolute discretion of the crown. He also disagreed with Churchill's reading of such a transfer. He said that resentment would continue in Ireland at what would appear to be "the unseemly obduracy of the British government". He reminded Churchill of their private exchanges on the matter and commended Churchill's initial reaction, which he described as natural, human and right.

During the next Dail session there was reference, in a polemical way to the visit, by one Deputy Oliver Flanagan of Fine Gael. He had asked the Taoiseach if he would protest to Churchill about a message he had sent to the Prime Minister of Northern Ireland. When the reply said that 'a protest would serve no useful purpose', Flanagan said, 'Has the Taoiseach ceased to send such protests since he was given the latchkey to and hospitality at number ten Downing Street... wining and dining with the British. Does the Taoiseach remember his charges of twenty years ago?'

At the end of 1953 Churchill was awarded a Nobel Prize, though not the Peace Prize he coveted, but one for literature and history. He retired as Prime Minister in 1955 and made his last appearance in the Commons on 28 July 1964, aged eighty nine years. He died in January 1965 after another stroke and was buried on 30 January. Ten Heads of State with representatives of one hundred and twelve countries attended the funeral at St. Paul's Cathedral in London. A large delegation, including Prime Minister Terence O'Neill, and the

Governor-General, attended from Northern Ireland. The Republic was represented by the Minister for External Affairs, Frank Aiken. Churchill was buried at the ancestral home of the Marlboroughs, Blenheim Palace.

Many tributes were paid to Churchill in Ireland. The Protestant Archbishop of Dublin, Dr. George Otto Simms, conducted Morning Service at St. Patrick's Cathedral, in his memory. Trinity College Dublin's Historical Society, where in 1902 Churchill had 'convulsed the House with merriment at his witticism at the expense of the traditional methods of English Party government', hoisted a large black flag to half-mast on Dublin's College Green. Mr. WT Cosgrave issued a tribute as did Taoiseach Sean Lemass. Mr. James Dillon, who alone of Dail TD's opposed Ireland's neutrality during the war, said, quoting Churchill's own words, 'It only remains for me to express to the British people, for whom I have acted in these perilous years, my profound gratitude', added his own: "This will serve as the most apt epitaph for a great public servant. When Nazism and Communism combined in 1939 to destroy freedom, his was the leadership which preserved it. Let us hope when Communism tries again, the generation of that day will produce as fearless a champion of freedom".

Eamon DeValera was by that time President of Ireland. There was much expectation about what he would say about his old foe. From next door to the Little Lodge, where Winston spent his boyhood years, DeValera issued this statement from the old Vice-Regal residence and then home to Irish Presidents, Aras An Uachtarain:

"Sir Winston Churchill was a great Englishman, one of the greatest of his time, a tower of strength to his own people and to their allies in their hour of need. For this he will be acclaimed throughout the world.

But we in Ireland had to regard Sir Winston over a long period as a dangerous enemy. The fact that he did not violate our neutrality during the war must always stand to his credit, though he indicated that in certain circumstances he was prepared to do so. In this connection I think I cannot do better than repeat a passage from a broadcast I made at the end of the war;

"By resisting his temptation in this instance Mr. Churchill instead of adding another horrid chapter to the already bloodstained record of relations between England and this country, has advanced the cause of international morality an important step - one of the most important indeed that can be taken on the road to the establishment of any sure basis for peace,

We sympathise with his widow and with all the members of Sir Winston's family in their bereavement and we hope that the 'mutual comprehension' between the peoples of these two islands for which Sir Winston prayed, may ultimately be realised".

In summation, various British governments, from the early years of this century, realised that the 1800 Act of Union between Great Britain and Ireland, was a mistake. They wished to revoke it and return a Parliament to Ireland. Even such an Imperialist as Winston Churchill, came to this view. But for reasons of self-interest and self-protection, the Unionists of the north eastern counties of Ireland, aided by allies within the Conservative Party, frustrated this government objective. Churchill sympathised with the Unionist position and buttressed the new Northern Ireland State. At the same time he was ensuring that the new Irish Free State became a reality. But he hoped and wished that at some future time, Ireland would again have one Parliament, with the agreement of all its people.

SOURCES

The main sources are the varied works of Winston Churchill himself, and the six volume life of "Winston S. Churchill" with its Companion Volumes written by Randolph Churchill and Martin Gilbert and published by Heinemann of London. Hansard was also a main source. Other sources are listed in the first chapter only in which they occur.

CHAPTERS

1.

My Early Life Winston Churchill Thornton Butterworth 1930
Jennie Anita Leslie Hutchinson 1969
Churchill Ted Morgan Jonathan Cape 1983
Ireland Simce the Famine FSL Lyons Fontana 1986

2.

Winston & Clementine Richard Hough Bantam Press 1990
Major John MacBride 1865-1916 Anthony Jordan Westport Historical Society 1991
Morning Star

3.

Standard-Conservative 19/2/1901 Report on Imperial Parliament.
Winston Churchill Henry Pelling MacMillan 1974

4.

Asquith Roy Jenkins London 1964
The Times 14/9/1910.
Asquith to King 7/2/1912. Ms.Asq.6.Fos 95-6.
The Times 13/9/1913.
Asquith Stephen Kos Allan Lane 1976
Daily Telegraph 9/10/1913

Freeman's Journal 13 & 20 October 1913.
Nation 11 & 18 October 1913
Guardian 20/10/1913.

5.

Lloyd George's Memo,Points discussed at dinner at 11 Downing St.
12/11/1913. L.G'S Papers c/4/1/10.
The Times 28/11/1913.
John Redmond Stephen Gwynn London 1932 Simon's Memo 10/3/1914
P.R.O. Cab. 37/119/46.
The Times 16/3/1914.
Glascow Herald 8/7/1914.

6.

Dardanelles Commission Report P.R.O.
New York Times December 1918.

7.

Illustrated Herald 13/6/1920.
Whitehall Diary Thomas Jones Oxford University Press 1971.
Memo 'The Irish Situation' 3/11/1920 CAB 23/23.
Daily Telegraph 4/11/1920.
The Times 15/1/1921
CAB 23/23 29/12/1920.

8.

L.G. Folio 14/6/5/ 8/7/1921.
Irish Times 9/7/1921.
Lloyd George to King 14/7/1921 L.G.F. 29/4/57.
CAB 23/26
DeValera Papers Dublin 1992.
Britain & Ireland 1914-23 Sheila Lawlor Gill & MacMillan 1983

9.

Churchill: A Study in Failure 1900-1939 Robert Rhodes James Weidenfeld & Nicholson 1970

Michael Collins Rex Taylor London 1958
Griffith to President, 31/10/1921 NP P7A/72
Collins to AG 31/10/1921: NP P7A/72.
Chamberlain to P.M. 11/11/1921.
Dail Cabinet 3/12/1921.
L.G.Folio F/25/2/51 & Jones to P.M. 2/12/1921.
The Last Lion William Manchester London 1983
Ireland and the Crown Brendan Sexton Irish Academic Press 1989

10.

Curtis Memo 18/3/1922 Colonial Office Papers(CO) 7/39/4.
Collins to M/D 14/3/1922: NP P7B/191.
Ireland 1912-1985 Joseph Lee Canbridge University Press 1990.
Death in Dublin - Michael Collins and the Irish Revolution Frank O'Connor Doubleday 1937
Mary Soames BBC TV Biography of Churchill 15/1/1992.

11.

CAB 23/30 5/4/1922.
Michael Collins Tim Pat Coogan Hutchinson
Collins to Churchill 5/6/1922 CO 906/21
Cope to Churchill 5/6/1922 CO 906/21.
Churchill & Ireland Mary C. Bromage University of Notre Dame 1964
State Paper Office Dublin S 1322/2 22/6/1922.
Clementine Churchill Mary Soames Cassell 1979
Sean MacBride Anthony Jordan Blackwater 1993
CAB 25/6/1922 11.30. 21/255.

12.

Provisional Government Minutes 27/6/1922
State Paper Office Dublin
CO 906/21 28&29/6/1922.
Churchill to Collins 29/6/1922.
CO 906/21.
Cope to Curtis 28/6/1922. CO 906/21.
Poblacht na hEireann War News 29/6/1922.

The Unsolved Question Nicholas Manseragh Yale University Press 1993
Concerning Winston Churchill George Arthur Kinsey New York 1941
Churchill to Cosgrove 25/10/1922 CO 906/22
Cosgrove to Churchill 8/9/1922 CO 906/22.
Provisional Government Minutes 3/10/1922 SPO.
Stanley Baldwin H.Montgomery Hyde Hart-Davis MacGibbon 1973
BBC TV January 1992 Biography of Winston Churchill.
Dundee Courier 17/11/1922.
New York Times 20/11/1922

13.

Brendan Bracken Charles Lysaght Allan Lane 1979
The Times 26/9/1924.
Birkenhead Papers 3/12/1925
Belfast Telegraph 4/12/1925
The Times 3/3/1926.

14.

The Restless Dominion DW Harness London 1969
Daily Mail 15/2/1933.
Dail Debates 27/4/1932.
DeValera Lord Longford & TP O'Neill Dublin 1970 Dail Debates 1-12/12/1936.
Churchill Papers 9/133 9/12/1938.
DeValera & The Ulster Question 1917-73 John Bowman Oxford University Press 1982
Irish Times 25/7/1934.
Roosvelt Papers PSF 56 Gray to Roosvelt 8/4/1940.

15.

Daily Telegraph 24/3/1939.
Dail Debates September 1939.
CAB 24/10/1939.
PRO CAB 65/1 WM 58(39)8.
Halifax Papers FO 800/310 Churchill to Eden 20/10/1939.
Churchill to First Sea Lord 5/9/1939

The Times 17/5/1939.
Curtis Papers Ms 90: Curtis Memo to Bevin.
PRO PREM 4/53/2 18/6/1940.
PRO 25/6/1939 Chamberlain Memo.
PRO PREM 6/7/1940 Craig Memo 'All Ireland Defence Force'.
Documents on German Foreign Policy VII 1956,422.
State Archives Dublin.
Irish Press 6/11/1940.
Dail Debates 6/11/1940.
PRO Northern Ireland CAB 21/5/1941.
Irish Press 23/5/1941.
Fuehrer Conferences on Matters...Navy 1940 Vol II pp.59-67.
Irish Press 28/1/1942.
Roosvelt Papers PSF 56.
USA State Department Bulletin 11/3/1944.
Irish News 14/5/1945.
Irish Press 17/5/1945.
Randolph Churchill to Frank Gallagher: Gallagher Papers. National Library Ireland. Ms 18 375(6) p.50a.
In Time of War Robert Fisk 1983.
Haughey Bruce Arnold Harper Collins 1993.

16.

Magill January 1983.
PRO CAB 18/1/1949.
Dail Debates May 1949.
Winston Churchill Struggle For Survival 1940-65 Lord Moran Constable 1966
Twentieth Century Ireland: Nation and State Dermot Keogh Gill & MacMillan 1994.
Dail Debates 25/10/1953.
Irish Independent 25/1/1965.

INDEX

Admiralty,	41, 47, 59, 63
Aiken Frank	197, 199
Amery Leo	172
Anglo-Irish Treaty	100, 106, 121, 127
Aras an Uachtarain	77, 199
Attlee Clement	36, 169, 172, 189, 192
Asquith Herbert	25, 27, 29, 32, 33, 37, 44, 47, 48, 49, 52, 56, 57, 58, 59, 62, 64, 75, 93
Asquith Violet	41
Aylesford Lady	8
Aylesford Lord	8
Bait J.	44
Baldwin Mrs	156, 157
Baldwin Stanley	152, 160, 164
Balfour Arthur	24, 26, 27, 35, 45, 58
Balmoral	44
Barrymore Ethel	30
Barton George	85, 97
Beal na Blath	141
Beleek	126, 127, 128
Belfast Butcher	53
Beresford Lord	53
Bevin Ernest	172
Birkenhead Lord	71, 86, 90, 91, 152, 165
Birrell Augustine	32, 38, 39, 40, 51
Black and Tans	71, 72, 73, 74, 79
Blenheim	8, 42
Blood Sir Bindon	17, 30
Blunt Wilfred	28
Board of Trade	32
Boer War	19, 26, 63, 77, 87
Boland FH	197
Bonar Law Andrew	35, 40, 42, 43, 44, 45 48, 50, 53, 57, 58, 59, 63, 70, 81, 92, 93, 96, 145, 146, 151
Botha Helen	30
Botha Louis General	28
Boundary Commission	6, 91, 93, 108, 111, 113, 139, 151, 153, 155, 156
Brabazon Colonel	15
Bracken Brendan	151, 152, 160, 169, 170 173, 195
Brennan Robert	183, 186
British Empire	6, 39, 42, 82, 83, 88, 111, 120, 170, 190
Brockway Fenner	152
B Specials	114, 123, 154, 157
Buckingham Palace Conference	55
Buller General	20, 21, 26
Burke TH	12
Campbell-Bannerman Henry	27, 93
Carlton Club	146
Carson Edward Sir	40, 42, 46, 48, 49, 51, 54, 56, 57, 59, 63, 101
Carter RN	182
Casement Roger	197
Cavendish Mr.	13
Cecil Robert Lord	118
Celtic Park	39
Chamberlain Austen	53, 86, 92, 93
Chamberlain Joseph	6, 17, 19, 23, 24, 25, 26, 27, 48, 59
Chamberlain Neville	153, 166, 167, 168, 169 170, 174
Chanak	144, 145
Chancellor of Exchequer	47, 153, 154
Chartwell	76, 105, 117, 143, 153
Chequers	155, 156
Childers Diary	97, 99
Childers Erskine	85, 89, 97, 99, 149, 150
Churchill Blandford	8
Churchill Jennie	11, 13, 17, 76, 77
Churchill John Strange	13
Churchill Marigold	77, 104
Churchill Mary	40
Churchill Randolph	8, 9, 14, 15, 38, 191
Cockran Bourke	16, 20, 23
Collins Michael	67, 84, 89, 91, 92, 94, 96, 103, 114, 119, 127
Colonial Office	78
Colville John	177
Commonwealth	6, 94, 95, 162
Conscription	62, 177, 178
Cosgrave William T	142, 143, 146, 155, 158, 164, 199
Costello John A	192, 197
Craig Charles	69
Craig James Sir	69, 71, 79, 81, 94, 95, 106, 113, 116, 118, 123, 154, 155, 156, 157, 174, 175
Cromwell	12

Curragh Mutiny 52
Curzon Lord 62, 77, 101
Dail 94, 106, 161
Dardanelles 58, 131, 144
Dardanelles Commission 61, 62, 63
DeValera Eamon 6, 66, 70, 80, 81, 82, 83, 99, 106, 119, 123, 155, 160, 162, 165, 166, 170, 172, 175, 176, 180, 184, 185, 186, 188, 191, 194, 195, 198, 199
DeValera Papers 175
Devlin JG MP 55, 68, 74, 117
Dillon James 199
Dillon John MP 46, 59, 156
Disraeli 8, 13
Dominion Status 81, 161, 179
Dublin 9, 11, 14, 23, 36, 44, 94
Duggan Eamonn 97
Duke of Marlborough 8, 14
Dundee 29, 147, 149
Dundee Couier 148
Dwyer Ryle T 182
Easter Rising 1916 22, 62, 66
Edward King VIII 165
Eden Anthony 170, 172, 196
Eire 182, 194
El Alamein 181
Emo Park 12
Esmonde Lieut. Comdr. VC. 185
Empress of Britain 176
Everest Mrs 11, 12, 16
External Association 86
External Relations Act 165
Famine Fund 14
Feetham Judge 156
Fegen Capt. VC. 185
Fenians 7, 12
Ferdinand Archduke 56
Finnucane VC. 193
Fisher Lord 59
Fitzgerald Desmond 162
Flanagan Oliver J 198
Four Courts 120, 133, 134, 136, 137
Franco General 196
Frank Anne House 181
Free State Irish 5, 104, 120, 127, 131, 138, 143, 154, 171, 194, 200
Free Trade 26
French Sir John 52, 61, 67
Gaelic Athletic Association 151
Gallipoli 58, 59, 61, 145
Gavan Duffy George 97
George VI 165
Gladstone William 14, 15, 17, 29, 37, 102
Goodwood Races 17
Government of Ireland Act 1920 72, 80
Gough General 52
Gray David 168, 181, 182, 183
Greenwood Hammar 71, 86
Grey Edward 27, 32, 55
Griffith Arthur 19, 84, 96, 97, 103, 106, 119, 140, 147
Haldane Lord 27
Halifax Lord 172
Harrow 15
Hart General 21
Haughey Charles J 184
Hempel Dr. 183
Hitler 169, 179, 181
Home Rule 5, 35, 56, 57, 66, 97
Home Rule All Round 37
Hooligans The 25
Hozier Bill 77
Hozier Clementine 30, 62, 76, 77, 104, 105, 117, 147, 153
Imperial Parliament 161
Ireland 5, 6, 7, 14, 76
Ireland Act 1949 6, 66, 102
Irish Brigades 19, 20, 21, 22, 62
Irish Labour Party 139
Irish legacy 76
Irish Parliamentary Party 33, 56, 62, 66
Irish Republic 66, 85, 118
Irish Republican Army 106, 118, 121, 135, 163, 171, 178
Iron Curtain 189
Kemal Mustapha 144
Kitchener General 17, 18, 21, 24, 58, 59, 63
Jeune Lady 18
Jews 181
Joint Executive Authority 173
Jones Thomas 91
Joubert General 20
Keneally Lance-Corporal VC. 185
Kennedy Joseph Ambassador 168
Lake Lugano 30
Laski Harold 94
Laurence TE (of Arabia) 148
Lemass Sean 199
Leslie Shane Sir 72
Little Lodge 7, 9, 10, 13, 23
Lloyd George David 24, 27, 30, 32, 34, 40, 41, 43, 47, 48, 49, 50, 58, 59, 63, 64, 69, 70, 75, 80, 82, 86, 90, 94, 103, 119, 127, 144, 146, 156
Londonderry Lord 37, 116
Lynch Arthur MP 20, 22
Lytton Pamela 143

MacBride John	19, 20, 22, 36, 62, 87
MacBride Gonne Maud	134
MacBride Sean	134, 191, 192
MacDonald Ramsay	160, 164
MacDonald Malcolm	174, 175, 186
MacEoin Sean General	108, 130
MacMahon Family Murders	114, 115
MacMillan Harold	169
MacNeill Eoin	155
MacReady General	36, 70, 71, 72, 73, 82, 109, 134, 136
MacRory Cardinal	178
McGarrity Joseph	85
McKinley President	24
Maffey John Sir	177, 180, 183
Malakand Campaign	17, 18
Manchester	26, 28
Manchester William	150
Mansion House	66
Marshall Plan	182, 189, 192
Masterman Charles	36
Molotov	182
Montgomery General	181
Moran Lord	195, 196
Morley John	27
Mulcahy Richard	142
Munich Agreement	169
NATO	195
Neutrality	170, 171, 176, 180, 181
Northern Ireland	106, 118, 121, 135, 163, 171, 178
Oath of Allegiance	94, 163, 164
O'Connell Ginger	136
O'Connor Rory	121, 124, 133, 137
O'Connor TP MP	45, 46
O'Higgins Kevin	116, 142, 143, 156, 157, 158
O'Neill Terence	198
Operation Overlord	183
Paget General	51
Pankhurst Emily	148
Parliament Bill	34
Pearl Harbour	179, 180
People's Budget	32, 47
Peter the Painter	35, 36
Pettigo	126, 127, 128
Phoenix Park	7, 9, 10, 12, 67
Plowden Pamela	30
Plunkett Count	85
Portarlington Lord	12
Prince of Wales	8, 18, 103
Provisional Government	103, 110, 119, 126, 136, 143
Queens University	159
Reading Without Tears	12
Redmond John	37, 43, 45, 50, 56, 57, 61, 156
Repington Colonel	59
Roberts Lord	21, 51
Robinson President	77
Rommel	181
Roosvelt President	24, 168, 176, 177, 180, 181
Rosebury Lord	17, 25
Salazar Antonio	196
Salisbury Lord	16, 18, 157
Sandhurst	15
Sarajevo	55, 56
Seely Jack	26, 51, 52
Shaw George Bernard	191
Simms George Otto	199
Simpson Wallis	165
Sinn Fein	19, 65, 66, 67, 68, 71, 73, 75, 79, 80, 99
Smuts Jan	28, 80, 81
St. Patrick's Cathedral	13, 191
St. Paul's Cathedral	134, 198
Stalin	182
Statute of Westminster	161, 162, 165
Sudan Campaign	17, 18
Suffraggettes	148
Sydney St Siege	35
Tonypandy	36
Trinity College	80, 184, 199
Tudor General	71, 72
Twain Mark	24
Ulster Covenant	43
Ulster Hall	159
Ulster Pogrom	53
Ulster Unionists	37, 54, 55, 57, 79, 89, 92, 95, 191
Ulster Volunteers	51, 53
Vice-Regal Lodge	9, 23
Viceroy	8
Victoria Crosses	193
Victoria Queen	8, 18, 24
Victory in Europe Day (V.E.)	184
Wilderness Years	160
Wilson Henry Sir	64, 67, 71, 72, 73, 81, 108, 113, 126, 132, 133, 134